Getting Started in

INVESTMENT ANALYSIS

The *Getting Started In* Series

Getting Started in

INVESTMENT ANALYSIS

Warren Brussee

WILEY

John Wiley & Sons, Inc.

Copyright © 2009 by Warren Brussee. All rights reserved.

Published by John Wiley & Sons, Inc., Hoboken, New Jersey.
Published simultaneously in Canada.

No part of this publication may be reproduced, stored in a retrieval system, or transmitted in any form or by any means, electronic, mechanical, photocopying, recording, scanning, or otherwise, except as permitted under Section 107 or 108 of the 1976 United States Copyright Act, without either the prior written permission of the Publisher, or authorization through payment of the appropriate per-copy fee to the Copyright Clearance Center, Inc., 222 Rosewood Drive, Danvers, MA 01923, (978) 750-8400, fax (978) 750-4470, or on the web at www.copyright.com. Requests to the Publisher for permission should be addressed to the Permissions Department, John Wiley & Sons, Inc., 111 River Street, Hoboken, NJ 07030, (201) 748-6011, fax (201) 748-6008, or online at http://www.wiley.com/go/permissions.

Limit of Liability/Disclaimer of Warranty: While the publisher and author have used their best efforts in preparing this book, they make no representations or warranties with respect to the accuracy or completeness of the contents of this book and specifically disclaim any implied warranties of merchantability or fitness for a particular purpose. No warranty may be created or extended by sales representatives or written sales materials. The advice and strategies contained herein may not be suitable for your situation. You should consult with a professional where appropriate. Neither the publisher nor author shall be liable for any loss of profit or any other commercial damages, including but not limited to special, incidental, consequential, or other damages.

For general information on our other products and services or for technical support, please contact our Customer Care Department within the United States at (800) 762-2974, outside the United States at (317) 572-3993 or fax (317) 572-4002.

Wiley also publishes its books in a variety of electronic formats. Some content that appears in print may not be available in electronic books. For more information about Wiley products, visit our web site at www.wiley.com.

Library of Congress Cataloging-in-Publication Data:

Brussee, Warren.
     Getting started in investment analysis / Warren Brussee.
          p. cm. — (The getting started in series)
     Includes index.
     ISBN 978-0-470-28384-4 (pbk.)
     1. Investment analysis.   I. Title.
     HG4529. B78 2009
     332.63'2042–dc22

                                        2008022844

Printed in the United States of America

10 9 8 7 6 5 4 3 2 1

This book is dedicated to Liam, Reed, Tess, Cara, and Emily.
I hope they grow up with a love of logic and the power of the word!

Contents

PART 1

LOOKING AT INVESTMENT DATA   1

PART 2

QUANTITATIVE DATA APPLICATIONS   37

Acknowledgments

I would like to thank Chris Welker, Roy McDonald, and Jeff Kolt for their valuable feedback on the initial manuscript. Like most writers, at some point in writing I become blind to my words, and I read what I *mean* to say rather than what I actually write. My reviewers shake me out of that fog with both their helpful suggestions and polite corrections. This book would not be possible without them.

Examples: Numerous examples illustrate points made in the discussion surrounding them and are designed to express ideas in practical terms.

Definitions: This symbol is found in boxed notations providing specific definitions of terms. These occur at the point of discussion with the book, making definitions to the section being read. (All definitions are also summarized for you in the glossary.)

Getting a Feel for Your Own Investments

People don't buy a car without looking at all viable options! Besides driving multiple cars, buyers generally get information on gas mileage and reliability. They then compare prices of the cars that make their final list. Sure, some emotion is part of the buying decision, but so is some real analysis of data. And, most likely, the buyer is using inputs other than those from the car dealers' salesmen.

In contrast, when people decide to invest, they often just give their money to a mutual fund or money manager with little review, or buy stocks with no idea of their real worth. They have been told by financial gurus to put their money into the stock market on a regular basis and watch it grow; don't sweat details like the price of stocks! Investors are told to just buy and hold, even though that isn't what money managers do.

The intent of *Getting Started in Investment Analysis* is to help people analytically kick the tires of potential investment options rather than just blindly buy stocks. This book won't enable everyone to pick stock winners, but it will make an investor more of an active participant in what to do with his or her hard-earned money. Very elementary examination of charts, identifying correlations, and doing simple statistical tests will give an investor some feel for the viability or risk of an investment.

There are thousands of publicly traded stocks available for purchase, and the positive aspects of these stocks are readily available in the communications released by each of the companies. Given this smorgasbord of stock choices, in addition to other investment options such as bonds and real estate, an investor can afford to be very selective. When in doubt, find another investment! That's why, on reading this book, at times it may seem that the bar on stock purchase is set very high. It should be! Due diligence should occur before you invest in anything. Consider the time and effort it took to save the investment funds versus the relatively little effort it takes to make sure those funds are invested wisely.

Approximately 50 percent of families own stocks, either through 401(k) savings plans, mutual funds, or individual stock purchases. Yet few people do their own critical evaluation of these investments or the economy. They trust other people to do this for them, even though those other people have obvious personal interests that may be in conflict with the investors'. *The priority of investment managers is their own financial gain, not that of the people whose funds they manage.* It would be wise to always keep that in mind.

Investment managers often supply misleading information related to their investments, striving to put their past performance in the best possible light. They periodically clean their stock portfolios so that the only stocks they own are those that have gone up in price. Sometimes investment firms just shut down poorly performing mutual funds so that their remaining funds all look good. They also compare their results with the S&P 500 stock index without including the dividends of the S&P 500, which is currently giving investment managers close to a 2 percent artificial advantage in their comparison.

Companies project future sales and earnings in the most optimistic light. They give glowing reports on future business opportunities while minimizing risks to their current businesses. In fact, Rate Financials, Inc., an independent research firm, estimates that one-third of the leading publicly traded companies do not accurately represent their financial condition. In their findings, only 4 percent of leading companies were rated outstanding in the publication of their finances.

Private firms' investment data are not the only data that may be suspect. Government information related to the economy is sometimes slanted to make the economy look better than it really is. For example, the government may emphasize the low core inflation rate, whereas the total inflation rate, the one that really affects us, is usually much higher.

Investors often have a difficult time determining whether their investments are doing better than the stock market in general or even beating inflation. Many investors have trouble telling whether a stock's price is changing because of random price variation or because of a meaningful change in a company's performance. They may even wonder whether they would be better off out of the stock market altogether, but the financial advice of so-called experts is to stick with stocks because, in the long run, these advisors promise that this is the only way to go!

This book uses simple data analysis to assist investors in making their investment choices. My earlier book, *Statistics for Six Sigma Made Easy,* simplified statistics for the data analysis related to Six Sigma, a problem-solving methodology used by many industries. Even though the Six Sigma process is often taught to engineers who have had statistics in college, most engineers do not regularly use statistics in their daily work. So it was necessary in *Statistics for Six Sigma Made Easy* to simplify the statistics so engineers could effectively use the Six Sigma methodology. *Getting Started in Investment Analysis* does the same for evaluating data related to investing. Even though some of the readers of this book may have taken statistics courses at some point in their education, this book assumes you have no formal statistics or in-depth quantitative analysis training. My intent is to help investors make some overall judgment on the data related to their investments *without* doing complicated statistical analysis. But where it is necessary, the process is made as painless and straightforward as possible. Only high school math and access to Microsoft's Excel are needed to do all the analysis shown in this book.

Walter Isaacson, in his book *Einstein,* notes that Einstein's "success came from questioning conventional wisdom." In the investment book *The Only Three Things That Count,* by Fisher, Chou, Hoffman, and Cramer, it says that "the only way to beat the market is to know something that other investors don't." Although this book won't help you attain breakthroughs on the order of Einstein's or always enable you to know something that other investors don't, its methods will often help you see things in data that other investors miss, and it does this by helping you analyze good data. There is a saying in Six Sigma that "In God we trust; all others must bring data." In general, that is the sort of criteria to use in evaluating stocks or any other investment.

Recognizing Meaningful Changes in Valid Data

The first thing an investor must realize is that almost all data are biased. So the goal is to filter out the worst data and to adjust the remaining data to make it easier to analyze. For example, an investor often wants to know if a stock's price increase was meaningful and, if so, what caused that change. To determine this, the investor must separate random price changes from those changes with an assignable cause, like a promising new product. This will put the investor in a much better position to judge whether the price change is likely to continue.

One of the ways to start identifying underlying causes of change is to correlate related data by using historical charts. However, even if multiple changes do correlate, investors must still satisfy themselves as to whether a likely cause-and-effect relationship exists. Only then can investors make the best judgment as to what is likely to happen in the future.

There is an oft-told story about mistaking correlation with true cause and effect. In the nineteenth century in Europe, someone documented a strong correlation between stork sightings and childbirths. Only later was it realized that the reason more storks were seen at the time of human births was that people stoked up their fireplaces as the birth times approached, which attracted the storks, who built their nests near the warm chimneys. Now, this did not make the correlation invalid. But if some other factor, like lack of food in the area, suddenly caused the storks not to come, the birth rate would not have been affected. There is always a temptation to assume that correlations prove cause and effect. Of course, that doesn't diminish the value of identifying correlations, since correlations are often the start of the process of identifying the true cause of an event.

Retirement Savings Have Unique Challenges

Many investment savings are for retirement. The last section of this book focuses on the very unique quantitative problems related to investing for and during retirement. What makes this such a challenge is that, besides the normal issues related to picking investments, we have to deal with the future value of money, how much money must be saved, minimizing risk, and how long someone is likely to live in retirement. And of course, we cannot ignore pension and Social Security issues, which affect investment needs.

Data Analysis

Microsoft's Excel is sufficient for all the analysis, graphing, and statistics used in this book. However, to do this analysis you must first make sure that Excel's Data Analysis is loaded into your computer. To verify this, bring up Microsoft's Excel on your computer. On the header on the top of the screen, click on Tools. A list of options will appear. If Data Analysis is one of them, then you are in fine shape! If not, under Tools, go to Add-Ins. Check the boxes for Analysis Toolpak and Analysis Toolpak VBA, then OK. If this is not available, you will have to insert the Microsoft Office Professional disk and install it. You may have to close and then reopen Excel to see Data Analysis as an option.

This book is useful without doing the data analysis shown because a lot of the concerns about investing are not quantitative. However, using Excel data analysis makes the process of picking investments far more robust and unemotional.

Summary of the Book's Goals

Getting Started in Investment Analysis will do the following:

- Show you how to critically judge the quality of stock or investment data and then separate the good data from the bad.
- Help you glean insights from valid investment data by using graphs and looking for correlations.
- Enable you to understand the additional complications related to retirement investing.
- Assist you in doing simple quantitative data analysis by utilizing Microsoft's Excel and high school mathematics.

Part

1

Looking at Investment Data

All data are suspect! Therefore, before any kind of quantitative analysis can be done, the data have to be validated. Wrong data must be discarded, misleading data corrected, and correct data cherished. Part 1 chapters give guidelines for and examples of this task.

Chapter 1: Getting Good Data

- Valid source
- Consistent source
- Consistent basis
- Real data (without inflation) versus regular data
- Manipulated data versus hard data (example: earnings versus dividends)

Chapter 2: Identify Visual Correlations

- Identify potential key process input variables (KPIVs)
- Incorporate time shifts (like inventory changes)
- Look for multiple correlations
- Can never prove cause with past data
- Inflation

Chapter 1

Getting Good Data

There are loads of data on investing and the economy. However, before using any of these data, investors must look at the source and the likely bias. Not that you should always ignore sources with a bias! Often an Internet source may have a viewpoint that is taken to an extreme, but the bias of that source may give you different insights and assist you in developing a more balanced view.

Let's first look at several important government economic measures related to the economy that many people think are misleading or just plain wrong. Since these government economic measures affect almost all stock prices, it is important to understand any bias in these numbers. When one of these numbers changes dramatically, most stocks are affected.

Consumer Price Index (CPI)

One economic indicator used by most investors is the CPI (Consumer Price Index), which is a measure of the cost of goods purchased by an average U.S. family. This is one of the key measurements for price inflation, which affects the value and prices of stocks dramatically. Many individuals and web sites take issue with the way the government calculates the CPI.

One popular contrarian web site assumes that *most* government statistics are erroneous, including the CPI, and the author of the site attempts to calculate what he

> **Consumer Price Index (CPI)**
> A measure of the cost of goods purchased by an average U.S. family

believes are the "real" statistics. His economic numbers are often far different than the government's. For example, as I am writing this, the government is showing a CPI, through August 2007, of 3.3 percent. The contrarian site maintains that if our government still calculated inflation the way it did in 1990, the CPI would be about 6.3 percent. And the site claims that if the CPI were calculated the same as in 1980, then the CPI would actually be over 10 percent! These are *huge* differences! So, are the much larger CPI numbers shown on the contrarian site correct, or are the government's numbers the right ones?

The government does acknowledge that it has made substantial changes in the way it calculates CPI. On the U.S. Bureau of Labor Statistics web site, all of this is explained. There is no attempt by the government to keep these changes secret. So, is the contrarian site correct that the real CPI is up to three times higher than what the government is saying?

Contrarian Web Site Bias

Let's look at the whole basis of the contrarian web site, which is to show that the government numbers are wrong! The contrarian site would have no readership, nor would its author be able sell his monthly newsletter, without the site showing dramatic discrepancies in the government's numbers. That doesn't necessarily mean that the site's author is wrong, but it should set off some alarms for you as to a possible bias in the numbers. Also, on some of the charts, the contrarian site compares what the site's author feels are the correct CPI numbers with the government's core CPI numbers. The core CPI does not include food or energy costs. Granted, the government uses the core CPI as one method to judge whether the country's inflation is excessive, but the government doesn't try to hide its calculated total inflation number, which, at the time I am writing this, is 1.8 percent more than the core inflation rate. Using the government's total inflation number would make up part of the discrepancy between the government's CPI number and the 1990 corrected numbers shown on the contrarian web site. The fact that the contrarian site chooses to compare apples and oranges (the government's *core* CPI versus the contrarian's corrected *total* CPI) should be a warning sign.

Continuing with the CPI question, another web site states that because the government's total CPI numbers show an increase of 3.3 percent through August (of the year I am writing this), if this is projected through the end of the year, this will be an annual inflation rate of 5.0 percent. This would be very high versus the CPI of recent years. Either out of carelessness, or by deliberately trying to mislead, the person who calculated this site's numbers ignored the fact that the government's 3.3 percent number is *already* an annualized rate, so what the web site was doing with its calculation makes no sense. The government is saying that, if the given rate of inflation continues, by the end of the year we will have experienced 3.3 percent inflation, *not* 5.0 percent. Again, this makes me suspicious of the data on this site.

Importance of CPI Accuracy

Let's continue with the CPI example because, to an investor, the CPI is important. If real inflation is actually higher than that reported by the government, then a rise in stock market prices could be largely due to inflation rather than to any real gain in stock value. Since the method of calculating inflation has changed dramatically, comparing stock prices before 1990 with those after 1990 may present issues, because the stock gain attributed to inflation may be understated in the periods after 1990. This knowledge could cause someone to consider investing mostly in stocks of commodities whose prices are closely related to real inflation rather than other stocks whose prices are not as closely tied to inflation. Also, it could suggest that someone should have minimum assets tied up in dollars, which would be losing value as real inflation builds.

Key Point
If real inflation is actually higher than that reported by the government, then a rise in stock market prices could be largely due to inflation rather than to any real gain in stock value.

CPI Variable Market Basket

To do investment analysis, it is important to understand what assumptions are included in the numbers used. Let's look more closely as to why the government chose to change its method of calculating CPI. Note that this examination of CPI requires no statistics, just a little time and a willingness to question the validity of data. The government changed its manner of calculating CPI in two ways. **First, the government uses a variable market basket, rather than a fixed market basket, to calculate CPI.** For example, if the price of green beans were to suddenly double because of some temporary cost related to the growing of beans, the current way of

Fixed Market Basket
An identical basket of goods whose cost change represents the rate of inflation

calculating CPI assumes that the purchaser will switch to some more affordable vegetable, such as broccoli or asparagus. This assumption of purchase change bothers some people who think that the comparison base line should not be changed. But the government did large surveys that showed that the consumer *does indeed do product substitution.* Consumers adjust what they buy based on cost, so their effective cost of living is somewhat leveled. This is the basis of the current CPI as determined by the government.

Key Point
To do investment analysis, it is important to understand what assumptions are included in the numbers used.

CPI Hedonistic Adjustment

The other change in calculating the **CPI includes what the government calls a hedonistic adjustment of price data, which assumes that the cost of any improvement in a product should be discounted when comparing it with an earlier price.** For example, a current automobile is likely to have safety features like antilock brakes and multiple air bags. If the government compared the cost of that current automobile with one that was purchased perhaps 20 years ago, it would make some allowance for the cost of these safety features that were not on the earlier automobile. In other words, the government's inflation assumption would be less than it would be if the two automobiles were assumed to be comparable. The government would adjust current prices downward in an attempt to make the automobile price comparisons more equivalent. Note that this is done even though in most cases it is impossible to buy a new car without the safety features. This same kind of cost adjustment is made on products like computers and other consumer goods. For example, if the computer you buy has higher speed and more memory than a similar computer purchased for the same price a year ago, the government's way of calculating inflation assumes that the price on the new computer actually went down because you are now getting much more computer for the same money. It doesn't matter if you really needed the increased speed and memory, or if it is even used.

Hedonistic Adjustment of Price Data
Assumes that the cost of any improvement in a product should be discounted when compared with an earlier price

Is the CPI Calculation Correct?

Because of the hedonistic adjustments, many economists think that *the CPI is understated by 1 to 2 percent*. However, most economists also believe that the previous CPI calculation method *overstated* inflation. The contrarian web site referred to earlier just assumed that the earlier ways of calculating CPI were correct and ignored the fact that the changes in the government's CPI calculations, at least as far as the variable market basket, were verified by surveys of actual consumer practices and the effect on their actual CPI.

In later chapters, when we are evaluating the stock market's historical performance without the effect of inflation, we have to keep in mind that, due to the apparent 1 to 2 percent understatement of current inflation, the recent real performance of the stock market is somewhat overstated versus the earlier market data. This kind of understanding is critical for quantitatively making judgments as to just how well the stock market is performing now compared with how it performed in the past.

Note that although some of the numbers on contrarian web sites seem biased, the sites *do* encourage readers to better understand the government's numbers and to make allowances for any discrepancy when doing investment analysis.

Unemployment Rate

Let's look at another critical number used in judging the economy: the unemployment rate. Every time the government updates this number, it is referred to by every financial news source; if it changes much, it is even discussed in the general news. But many people, based on what they see around them, think that the government's unemployment number is too low. So, let's try to get a better understanding of the unemployment number and the assumptions included. Again, this approach is required for doing meaningful investment analysis because a large change in the unemployment rate can affect stock prices dramatically.

Key Point

A large change in the unemployment rate can affect stock prices dramatically.

According to the U.S. Department of Labor web site, as I write this the unemployment rate is 4.6 percent. But if you look at the government web site's details, the 4.6 percent **unemployment rate does *not* include those who work**

part time because they can't get a full-time job and those who want a job but have given up looking. When those people are included, the unemployment number jumps to 10.3 percent! Note that the government doesn't hide this higher number; it just isn't the number that's widely publicized! But a lot of web sites and articles point to the 10.3 percent unemployment number as evidence of a slow economy and argue that the generally quoted 4.6 percent unemployment rate is misleading.

Is the Unemployment Number Misleading?

At the Department of Labor web site, you can see that historically there have always been a substantial number of people working part time (and not included in the unemployment rate) because they can't get a full-time job and others who wanted a job but have given up looking. And the government has not changed the way it calculates unemployment. So the government does *not* seem to be trying to mislead people into believing that the economy is healthier than it is by publishing the 4.6 percent unemployment rate. As I write this book, at least in comparison with the gross historical unemployment rate, the economy is doing well with unemployment! However, if the unemployment rate jumped substantially, it could portend a slowing economy with a resultant drop in stock prices.

Unemployment Change Significance

There is another valuable detail on the U.S. Department of Labor site. The government shares some of the statistics related to the unemployment number. In a nutshell, it says that a 0.1 percent change in unemployment is generally meaningless because of the inaccuracy of their numbers due to a relatively small sample size. In fact, the change in unemployment must be at least 0.2 percent before you have a reasonably high probability that the change is meaningful. And even then, there is a 10 percent chance that the change was just due to random error and actual unemployment didn't really change! A few months ago, when the government's published monthly unemployment rate rose from 4.5 percent to 4.6 percent, many financial news broadcasters said that unemployment was rising, and the stock market reacted negatively. But the change in unemployment was so small as to be statistically insignificant, and a wise investor would have ignored it!

Key Point
The change in unemployment must be at least 0.2 percent before there is a reasonably high probability that the change is meaningful.

Data Source

Any net site should reference the original source of data. An investor should then go to that referenced site to make sure that the data were not selectively chosen such that they no longer reflect the intent of the original source. Once the true source is identified, some judgment is still required as to the likely accuracy of the data. If the original data source is not identified, then the data should automatically be suspect. A lot of data on the Internet are just plain wrong!

Investors must be careful when comparing data from different sources. The baselines or time intervals of the multiple sets of data may be different. Even when comparing very specific data, like the performance of the S&P 500 or housing prices, you have to be sure whether inflation is included and identical time periods are represented. For example, let's say you want to know the median price of an existing single-family home sold in the United States in 2006 so you can compare it with the price of a comparable home in 2007. Looking at several apparently reputable sources for this information, I recently got the following median selling prices of existing single-family homes sold in the United States in 2006: National Association of Realtors, $221,900; *USA Today*, $230,000; *Real Estate Journal*, $222,000; American Land Title Association, $229,300. So I got a discrepancy of nearly 3.7 percent. Which number is correct? I don't know! On the sites, it looked as if all the prices represented the median existing single-family home sold in the United States in 2006. Perhaps if I sent an e-mail to each source and they sent me detailed information on how they calculated their values, I could find subtle differences on what was or was not included in their values. For example, maybe one value was the average of 12 months of 2006 whereas another number was as of the end of June 2006. The easiest solution is to make sure that whatever source used for the 2007 prices is the same source used for the 2006 numbers, since the assumptions and methods of calculation were probably the same for each year. If in doubt, do the same-source calculation separately for several different sources, and verify that you get similar results related to the amount of change between the two years.

Key Point

Investors must be careful when comparing data from different sources. The baselines or time intervals of the multiple sets of data may be different. Even when comparing very specific data, like the performance of the S&P 500 or housing prices, you have to be sure whether inflation is included and identical time periods are represented.

Managed Numbers

One thing to keep in mind when using numbers is the likelihood of those numbers being managed. Using numbers for investment analysis is worthless if the related data aren't truly representative. Some data are easy to manipulate, like company earnings. Other numbers, like dividends paid, are more definitive because they represent actual dollars paid out to investors. Let's look at several ways that companies manage earnings numbers so that they are not always representative of the real earnings of a company.

Key Point

Using numbers for investment analysis is worthless if the related data aren't truly representative. Some data are easy to manipulate, like company earnings. Other numbers, like dividends paid, are more definitive because they represent actual dollars paid out to investors.

Here is an example! Engineers' salaries, which had previously been expensed every year, are now included in the costs of the equipment they design, and their salaries are therefore depreciated with that equipment. This change will have a very positive effect on the implementation year's earnings. Its effect on the year of change is almost equivalent to eliminating much of the engineering group. (Actually, the effect is greater because there are no related layoff costs.) For a somewhat simplified example, assume an engineer is earning $100,000 per year and that salary is expensed in the current year. The $100,000 salary is subtracted from this year's earnings. However, starting the next year, if that engineer's salary is depreciated for 10 years along with the machine that engineer is designing, the bottom-line cost of that engineer for the year will be only $10,000! This change increases next year's published earnings by $90,000! Note that there is nothing illegal about doing this as long as all proper details of the accounting changes are duly noted in the company's financial reports. But earnings go up without any real improvement in the company; $90,000 of costs is just delayed into future years. And since many investors blindly look at earnings without going into enough detail to truly understand their character, investors are likely to bid up the stock's price with the same enthusiasm they would have if the improved earnings had come from a new product line or a product innovation. A new product or innovation would probably bring positive long-term potential for the company, so it would have been a much higher quality of earnings gain versus the delay in recognizing engineering costs.

In another example, pieces of equipment that are part of a series production line, such that each piece of equipment feeds the following piece of equipment, had previously been depreciated as individual stand-alone devices. However, someone now determines that no individual piece of this equipment has value as a stand-alone, so the whole series of equipment in the production line can be considered one large piece of equipment. The summed total value of all this equipment now qualifies for a longer depreciation period, reducing the net amount to be depreciated each year compared with the sum of each piece being depreciated separately. This lowers the depreciation costs in the year that the accounting change is implemented and increases earnings for that year. Again, nothing is illegal! The accounting change just delays costs into future years because the depreciation of the equipment would go on for additional years. There is no real long-term improvement to the company; in fact, future years would have a higher cost burden. The long-term cost burden is accompanied by a risk that the equipment will be obsolete well before its depreciation is completed, causing the company to either write off the remaining value or put the obsolete equipment in a warehouse filled with other equipment with depreciation left that no manager wants to recognize in any given year.

Another way a chief financial officer of a company can push out costs is by adjusting the provisions for inventory obsolescence, which is pretty subjective in any case. The CFO only has to justify this to an auditor who has less of an idea on how to value a pile of old parts than the company's CFO.

In the 1990s, many companies became very proficient at doing creative accounting similar to the examples given here. GE was typical of the companies that managed their earnings. Because of their superb reported earnings in the 1990s, GE's stock price reached $60 in the year 2000. As I am writing this book, GE stock is at $41, whereas the general market has recovered to year 2000 levels. Is the fact that GE pushed costs into the future just coincidence to their stock price now being rather dormant versus the general market? The delaying of costs by many companies in the late 1990s seems to have hurt recent earnings growth of these companies.

> **Chief Financial Officer (CFO)**
> The executive responsible for all the financial aspects of the company

So, anyone looking at company earnings data must keep in mind the possibility of the data being managed before making a judgment about how a company, or the overall economy, is doing. Earnings are easily manipulated.

Questioning Earnings Growth

It is not necessary for an investor to be aware of insider details to be suspicious of earnings growth. For example, a preliminary look at a company's sales growth may show that their earnings were growing at a far greater rate than their sales revenues. There can be very rational reasons for this difference, and it isn't always a bad thing. But investors should satisfy themselves that they understand the reasons.

As I write this in October 2007, here are some GE data from the previous several years.

- 2004 Revenue (millions of U.S. dollars) = 152,866 Net income per share = $1.60
- 2006 Revenue (millions of U.S. dollars) = 163,391 Net income per share = $2.01

So, revenues were up 6.89 percent over the previous three years while net income per share went up 25.63 percent. Before buying this stock, I would try to understand the basis for this earnings growth, given the relatively slow sales revenue growth. In coming chapters, we refer back to GE several more times to look at the company with additional analysis tools. GE works as a good model because it is often viewed as a stalwart example of American corporations; because of its broad range of product lines, it is considered indicative of the economy in general. Again, the intent is to show that an investor can make some judgment on the validity of data, even for a large corporation like GE. Applying the same kind of analysis will help investors make better judgments about their potential investments in other companies and in other investment options.

Company Management

The background of the CEO of a company can give someone a hint as to whether earnings are likely to be managed. Many high-level managers who thrived during the 1990s were trained in the art of optimizing earnings, even at the possible detriment of longer term company earnings. Many of these high-level managers went on to become the CEOs of corporations, and they brought their accounting wizardry with them. Examples are Jeff Immelt (CEO at GE), Jim McNerney (CEO at Boeing), and Bob Nardelli (CEO at Chrysler). They are primarily *money managers* who may emphasize quick fixes, outsourcing, and accounting magic rather than investing in long-term efforts to truly grow a business. Managers were very unlikely to get to the upper levels at GE and similar companies by being product or process innovators, because process and product development takes

Money Managers

Managers who emphasize optimizing quarterly profits rather than other aspects of running or building a company much more time, costs more, and has higher risks than postponing costs to the future or outsourcing to low-cost countries. The U.S. automotive manufacturing managers are poster children for how to bleed businesses rather than aggressively doing product innovation. And now the automotive companies and our country in general are paying the price.

Contrast this with the people running Microsoft or Apple. Their quarterly earnings are far more volatile because these companies emphasize what is needed to grow their businesses long term, not to meet or slightly exceed market expectations. True innovations don't give uniform quarterly payoffs! In fact, when you see very stable earnings growth for extended periods, you should suspect that the earnings are being managed.

Key Point

Managers who are skilled in short-term earnings optimization can often drive up their company's stock price quickly and dramatically. But investors should be prepared to exit these stocks as the short-term fixes run dry.

Managers who are skilled in short-term earnings optimization can often drive up their company's stock price quickly and dramatically. This practice is not necessarily bad, and investors can gain from it. But investors must also realize that this may not be the best path for long-term company growth, and investors should be prepared to exit these stocks as the short-term fixes run dry. Of course, if there is evidence of long-term growth along with cost control, then this situation is ideal!

Summary

We must learn to question all data, understanding the biases, assumptions, and significance. This is true for government, company, and Internet data. Most data that are published have had some previous editing, and the intent is often to mislead or at least to prejudice a conclusion.

- The CPI (Consumer Price Index) is probably understated 1 percent to 2 percent.
- The unemployment rate does not include people working part time (whether of their own volition or not) or those who have given up looking for jobs. A change in the unemployment rate of less than 0.2 percent has no statistical significance.

- Multiple data sources should be referenced for verification and consistency. If two sources use different baselines, don't compare data from these two sources without adjustment.

- Company earnings can easily be managed to give misleading indications of a company's real profits or potential. The background of the company's CEO can often give some hint as to the likelihood of this happening.

Chapter

Identify Visual Correlations

To start this chapter, we are going to look at an example of purchasing a restaurant, using charts to check for correlations. This example is a nice size contrast to the earlier GE discussion, and it shows how investment analysis works on all sizes and types of investments. People buying stocks should analyze their purchases with much the same kind of careful logic they would use if they were buying a small company. After all, when someone buys a share of stock in a company, they are buying a portion of that company. And people often have more money invested in their stocks than someone invests to buy a small business.

I also want to introduce a concept from Six Sigma, which is a problem-solving methodology used to study complex industrial processes. In industry, and when looking at investments, it is important not to get bogged down in all the small variables that are not likely to be important. Instead, the idea is to identify the key process input variables (KPIVs), the main drivers affecting change. The stock market, and even a small business, has many contributing elements, but you need to concentrate on the KPIVs.

> **Six Sigma**
> A problem-solving methodology that uses data to drive decisions

Identifying Key Variables Affecting a Restaurant Purchase

This restaurant example is based on a real event, but I have simplified the detail and numbers to make it easier to follow. A few years ago, a friend of mine, who had extensive experience in running a restaurant, asked me for assistance

Key Process Input Variables (KPIVs)

The main drivers affecting change; the stock market, and even a small business, has many contributing elements, but it is important to concentrate on the KPIVs

in determining whether buying a pizza restaurant in a small city near where we lived was a good investment. This friend had a business degree and felt competent in analyzing the financial statements, but he wanted impartial input on the viability of the venture as a whole. The person selling the restaurant was retiring, and he showed detailed historical data of the restaurant's profits and growth for its prior 10 years of operation. The pizza restaurant was very large and had the potential to handle many more customers. My friend and I observed that, with the relatively fixed costs of the restaurant building and utilities, a further increase in the number of customers should disproportionately increase profits. So, with simple logic, we identified that the number of restaurant customers was a KPIV affecting profits. A lot of other input variables may affect a restaurant's profits, but perhaps not as dramatically as the number of customers. The other key inputs could be the number of menu choices, menu prices, advertising dollars, number of competitors, additional competitors, and competitor actions, but it was important for us to use some judgment in limiting the list of KPIVs to analyze; otherwise, we would get overwhelmed with data. I knew that if we picked a wrong KPIV, we could easily tell because there would be no correlation with earnings.

We looked at three KPIVs, making a chart of each. The first was historical profits per quarter, the second was the number of customers per quarter, and the third was area population growth by quarter. Comparing the first two charts, we expected that there would be a correlation, with profits growing somewhat at a higher rate than customer growth because of the relatively fixed cost of the restaurant building. Although we didn't expect any surprises in these two charts, we wanted to validate that the number of customers was a KPIV.

Of course, what we really wanted to know was the likelihood of the business and its profits continuing to grow, because otherwise we wouldn't consider the restaurant a good investment. We were aware that the area in which the restaurant was centered was growing in population, with several large housing developments having been built in the previous 10 years. We wanted to see, by comparing the past restaurant customer growth with the area population growth, if there was a correlation. If we saw a correlation, we would then try to make some judgment as to the future, at least related to the continuing growth of the area's population.

Using Excel to Make Charts or Graphs

Before we look at the three charts that were generated for the restaurant example, let's briefly go through the steps of making simple charts or graphs with Excel. Bring up Excel on your computer. Copy the numbers from Table 2.1 into Excel's columns A through F. There are 40 values in each column of numbers. In Excel, under each column of numbers, you can name each column so you can easily refer back to them. The numbers in column B are the restaurant's "profits," column D is the restaurant's number of "customers," and column F is the "population" of the immediate area. The other columns are dates.

TABLE 2.1	Restaurant Profits, Customers, and Area Population per Month				
A	B	C	D	E	F
Month-Year	Net Profits	Month-Year	Customer	Month-Year	Population
Mar-96	35,667	Mar-96	31,067	Mar-96	63,927
Jun-96	34,885	Jun-96	28,645	Jun-96	63,988
Sep-96	38,520	Sep-96	30,573	Sep-96	64,834
Dec-96	37,811	Dec-96	32,989	Dec-96	64,745
Mar-97	39,421	Mar-97	32,483	Mar-97	65,836
Jun-97	43,976	Jun-97	37,656	Jun-97	76,047
Sep-97	47,074	Sep-97	41,878	Sep-97	82,116
Dec-97	49,854	Dec-97	43,528	Dec-97	88,788
Mar-98	53,736	Mar-98	49,363	Mar-98	98,911
Jun-98	54,360	Jun-98	49,174	Jun-98	99,124
Sep-98	55,124	Sep-98	48,526	Sep-98	99,328
Dec-98	56,333	Dec-98	49,100	Dec-98	99,566
Mar-99	55,989	Mar-99	51,626	Mar-99	100,018
Jun-99	56,432	Jun-99	50,787	Jun-99	99,898
Sep-99	56,843	Sep-99	50,332	Sep-99	100,385
Dec-99	58,432	Dec-99	52,645	Dec-99	101,744
Mar-00	58,759	Mar-00	50,225	Mar-00	102,666
Jun-00	57,391	Jun-00	51,111	Jun-00	102,375
Sep-00	57,313	Sep-00	54,367	Sep-00	104,890
Dec-00	58,686	Dec-00	52,858	Dec-00	103,639
Mar-01	59,004	Mar-01	53,241	Mar-01	103,822
Jun-01	59,342	Jun-01	54,345	Jun-01	105,287
Sep-01	60,531	Sep-01	52,121	Sep-01	104,749

(continued on next page)

TABLE 2.1 (Continued)

A Month-Year	B Net Profits	C Month-Year	D Customer	E Month-Year	F Population
Dec-01	60,659	Dec-01	53,926	Dec-01	105,121
Mar-02	61,231	Mar-02	53,177	Mar-02	105,294
Jun-02	61,632	Jun-02	53,725	Jun-02	107,121
Sep-02	60,979	Sep-02	55,942	Sep-02	113,747
Dec-02	64,862	Dec-02	57,354	Dec-02	117,339
Mar-03	67,499	Mar-03	62,125	Mar-03	128,774
Jun-03	71,534	Jun-03	70,722	Jun-03	133,212
Sep-03	73,423	Sep-03	68,458	Sep-03	136,222
Dec-03	76,989	Dec-03	68,444	Dec-03	141,009
Mar-04	81,645	Mar-04	71,388	Mar-04	146,880
Jun-04	85,125	Jun-04	71,968	Jun-04	154,554
Sep-04	84,529	Sep-04	73,247	Sep-04	155,277
Dec-04	84,522	Dec-04	74,255	Dec-04	155,863
Mar-05	86,977	Mar-05	75,124	Mar-05	156,323
Jun-05	86,487	Jun-05	77,642	Jun-05	155,499
Sep-05	92,488	Sep-05	74,266	Sep-05	155,742
Dec-05	93,745	Dec-05	78,919	Dec-05	157,874

Highlight the column A and B numbers by clicking on the cell with the number in the top left corner and then holding your mouse key down as you move across and then down the columns until you highlight all the numbers. Then take your finger off the mouse key. All the numbers in columns A and B should now be highlighted. In the header at the top of the Excel worksheet, click on "Insert," then "Chart." For "Chart Type," pick "Line." For this example, I used the lines with diamonds at each value point. Double-click on the diagram that matches your preference. A window then comes up showing your chart. Click on "Next" at the bottom of this window. You now have a chance to enter a chart title, where I entered "Restaurant Profits." You then can enter a category (X) axis, where I entered "Year by Quarter." And you can enter a value (Y) axis, where I entered "Dollars." When you are done, click on "Next" at the bottom of the screen. On the next window, choose "As New Sheet," then click on "Finish" at the bottom of the screen. You now see your finished chart. Print this chart so you can compare it with the additional charts that you are going to create from the other columns on your Excel spreadsheet. Figure 2.1 is this first chart.

If you look at the bottom of your chart on your computer screen, you will see boxes labeled Chart 1 and Sheet 1. Click on "Sheet 1," which shows your

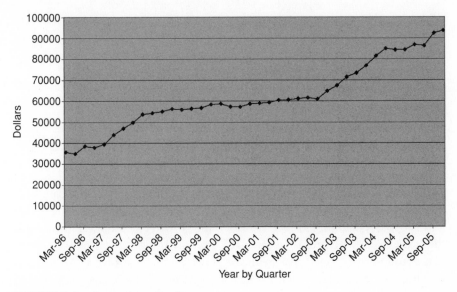

FIGURE 2.1 Restaurant Profits

spreadsheet data. Highlight the numbers in columns C and D, and repeat the same process you just did for columns A and B, but this time name the chart "Restaurant Customers," and label the (Y) axis "Number." Figure 2.2 is the resultant graph, which you should again print out for reference.

At the bottom of your chart on your computer screen are boxes labeled Chart 1, Chart 2, and Sheet 1. Click on "Sheet 1," which shows your spreadsheet

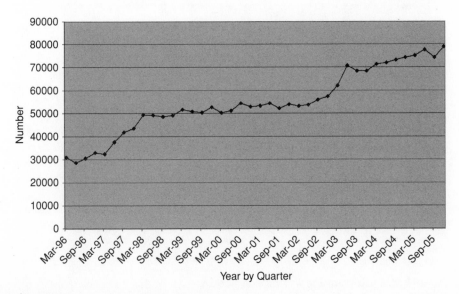

FIGURE 2.2 Restaurant Customers

data again. Highlight the numbers in columns E and F and repeat the same process you just did for columns A and B and C and D, but this time name the chart "Restaurant Region Population," with the (Y) axis "Number." Figure 2.3 is the resultant graph, which you should again print out for reference.

All three charts could be combined into one chart, but I kept everything as simple as possible for this example.

Comparing Figure 2.1 and Figure 2.2

By comparing Figures 2.1 and 2.2, you can see that, as expected, there is a good correlation. The number of restaurant customers does strongly correlate with earnings. That means that the number of customers appears to be a KPIV affecting the restaurant's profits. However, the growth of earnings in this period did not exceed the customer growth (157 percent) until the last two quarters. We would have expected that, with the relatively fixed costs of the restaurant building, we would have seen the earnings shown in the last two quarters at least two years earlier. When we asked the owner about this, he explained that it just took a while to get waitresses trained and so forth. But the jump in earnings was so sudden in the last two quarters that we felt that this explanation was not sufficient.

When visiting the restaurant, we decided to see if we could better understand this jump in profits. While there, we happened to have a waitress who had been working there for a few years. We remarked that it looked like a good place to work. She agreed but said that it had not always been that way. When

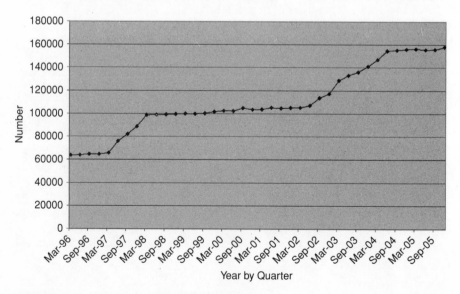

FIGURE 2.3 Restaurant Region Population

we asked why, she explained that, as is true for most restaurants, when the owner or a qualified manager was not in attendance, the restaurant help were less attentive to customers and the general feel of the restaurant deteriorated. She noted that, for the half last year or so, the owner "seemed to almost live here; he never went home."

We then understood what had happened for the last six months. Because the owner was planning to sell, he was doing whatever was required to maximize profits. Since my prospective partner, who was going to run the restaurant, didn't plan to "live" at the restaurant, we knew that he would have to hire several qualified (and costly) managers to be there when the owner wasn't, which would reduce overall profits. Note that this observation of requiring additional management initially came from examining charts and trying to understand inconsistencies in correlations, and the follow-up at the restaurant gave us the needed detail.

Comparing Figure 2.2 and Figure 2.3

When comparing Figures 2.2 and 2.3, we also see a strong correlation. In fact, the growth of the region population (147 percent) appears to account for most of the increase in the restaurant's customers (157 percent). Note that I said "appears to" account for the increased number of customers. Correlations can never prove cause and effect. They can only give hints, and judgment must be used to make any decisions about these correlations. In an industrial process, controlled experiments can be used to test cause and effect to a high confidence level by controlling variables other than the KPIV of interest. But controlled tests are seldom feasible in evaluating investments because you cannot control the other input variables. So other methods must be used, including logic and analyzing multiple sources.

Key Point
Correlations can never prove cause and effect. They can only give hints. Judgment must be used to make any decisions about these correlations.

Now, here is how my friend got the real benefits of going through these efforts. He reviewed recent meeting notes from the region's zoning board and found that zoning was no longer being approved for large housing projects. There had been two large housing development programs submitted within the last year, and the zoning board had turned down both. The reason given by the board was that the existing infrastructure, such as roads, water, sewer, and schools, could not support any more growth. There was talk of growing this infrastructure, but my friend realized that this may not happen, and in any case, it would probably be many years in the future. In the meantime, the restaurant's earnings growth could be stymied. And with the asking price for the restaurant seemingly based on continuing growth (the owner would not reduce the price when he was confronted with the zoning board information), the purchase no longer seemed like a good investment. In this case, the investigation of the KPIV of population growth, which seemed to account for much of the past growth, indicated that future growth of restaurant customers could be slow. Sure, someone who wanted to bet on expanding the restaurant's menu or upgrading the facilities might be able to grow the restaurant's profits despite the area's lack of population growth, but my friend and I agreed that this made the restaurant investment too risky, especially given the price.

Readers should have gleaned several things from this example. First, some simple analysis of data helped us make an investment decision. Second, checking for correlations hinted that population growth had been a primary driver in past restaurant profit growth, and that drove us to find that future population growth was not expected, at least not soon. And third, the price of the restaurant was an important part of the investment decision. At a lower price, the restaurant may have been a good investment even without the population growth, but it was not a good buy at the current price. Few investors give their stock investment picks even the rudimentary overview that we gave the pizza restaurant purchase, especially related to price!

Key Point

First, some simple analysis of data helped us make an investment decision. Second, checking for correlations hinted that population growth had been a primary driver in past restaurant profit growth, and that drove us to discover that future population growth was not expected, at least not in the immediate future. And third, the price of the restaurant was an important part of the investment decision.

How Applicable Is This Analysis?

Dividends
A distribution of corporate earnings

Many readers at this point may be wondering how useful this kind of analysis is for large-company stocks, such as those on the S&P 500. Well, let's look again at GE, which a few years ago had a higher total stock value than any other company in the world. We already mentioned several ways that GE may have managed earnings. But was there anything in GE's stock price that should have alarmed investors who weren't aware of all these details?

First, in Figure 2.4, I show a graph of the proportional change of the S&P 500 Index every six months. I used values that include adjustments for dividends (assumes that dividends are reinvested) and splits.

Then, in Figure 2.5, I graphed the proportional change of GE every six months. I again used values that include adjustments for dividends and splits.

Comparing Figures 2.4 and 2.5, it isn't easy to see much except that GE seems to be generally higher and very uniform in the six-month change average in the later part of the 1990s. So I generated another chart, Figure 2.6, showing the GE change rate minus the S&P 500 change rate to try to see more that's of interest.

Again, it is difficult to see much. But on the right-hand side of the graph, near the end of the 1990s, there are seven points in a row (with the highest point on the chart right in the middle of the seven points) that are mostly positive, which seems to be unique for the graph time period.

Going back to the raw data used to build the graph, I found that those are the periods between July 1998 and June 2001. So, let's see if we can get more information from this data by looking at the average differences

Splits

A company increases the number of its shares, and the price then adjusts down-ward in the same propor-tion; the net equity of each shareholder after a stock split generally stays the same

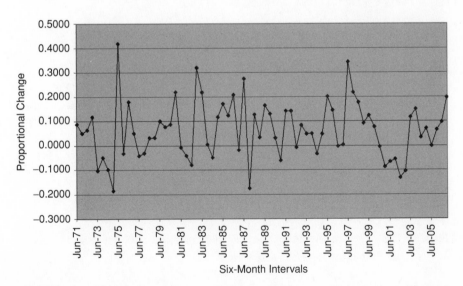

FIGURE 2.4   Proportional Change in S&P 500 Index (Adjusted for Splits and Dividends), Six-Month Intervals

Source: Data from http://finance.yahoo.com/

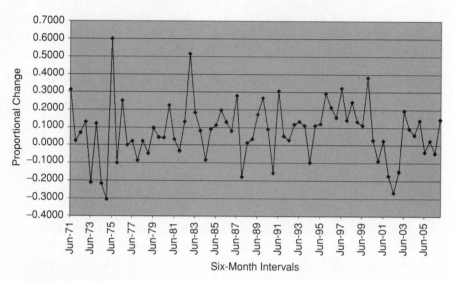

FIGURE 2.5   Proportional Change in GE Price (Adjusted for Splits and Dividends), Six-Month Intervals

Source: Data from http://finance.yahoo.com/

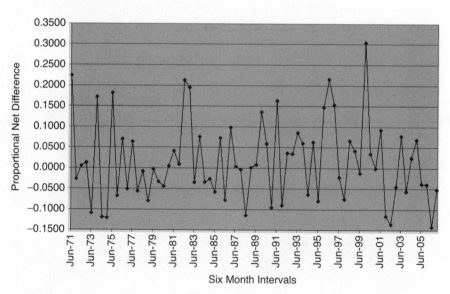

FIGURE 2.6   Net Change in Difference: GE Minus S&P 500, Six-Month Intervals

Source: Data from http://finance.yahoo.com/

between GE and the S&P 500 for the period between July 1998 and June 2001 versus the time intervals before and after those dates. I illustrate this in Figure 2.7.

With this graph, it becomes evident. In the period before June 1998, the GE stock price gain, including dividends, averaged 2.1 percent per six-month interval (4.2 percent annually) higher than the S&P 500, including dividends. That is a good performance! However, starting July 1998, GE really took off, with its stock, including dividends, performing at an unbelievable 7.5 percent average increase per six-month interval (15.6 percent annually) in excess of the average performance of the S&P 500. And since the S&P 500 was going up an average of 4.5 percent per six-month interval (9.2 percent annually) during that period, the average gain for the GE stock price between July 1998 and June 2001 was almost 25 percent per year!

However, following this remarkable period, the average GE price change plus dividend results have been almost 4.1 percent per six-month period *less* than the S&P 500 average including dividends. Since the S&P 500 was going up approximately 4.0 percent per six-month period during this most recent time interval, that means that GE was basically flat and actually losing real value every year since June 2001 when inflation is included!

When we revisit the data used to generate Figure 2.7, statistical tests on the raw data can determine whether the three different levels shown visually on the graph are statistically different or just random events.

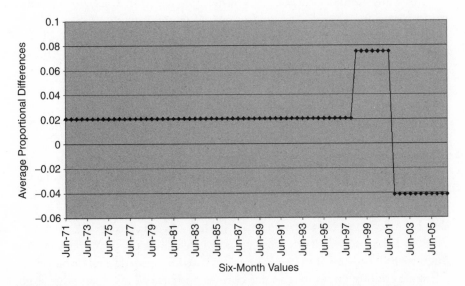

FIGURE 2.7 Six-Month Interval Average Differences: GE Minus S&P 500, June 1971–June 1998, July 1998–June 2001, July 2001–December 2006

Source: Data from http://finance.yahoo.com/

Questioning GE's Performance

Just as with the pizza restaurant example, investors should have been questioning the superb GE performance during the July 1998 to June 2001 period. Granted, during this same time period, the price of many tech-bubble stocks went up a remarkable amount. But GE, with its size and diverse product lines, is like a huge ocean liner. Unlike many companies, GE's products are so diverse that it would be impossible for any one or two innovations to affect GE so dynamically across their entire product universe. It is not easy to accelerate or change GE's momentum, so the change had to be significant and very identifiable. It was! Jack Welch, GE's CEO, dictated cost reductions and insisted on superb earnings performance across the company. And to get the expected results, GE divisions often came up with creative accounting changes. Yes, there were also great innovations, but not of a size or compass to drive such a remarkable earnings jump across the company.

Was it possible for outside investors to have an idea what was going on within GE? Sure! As I have said, just the fact that such a dramatic change took place in such a large and historic company should have given investors pause. And Jack Welch was featured in many articles that praised his management methods. There was no great invention that was driving these increased profits. In fact, the GE sales volumes during this period were growing only at the same rate they were before the remarkable share price jump.

But how would someone know when the great GE stock price performance was going to end? The kind of savings going on within GE could not continue forever, but obviously no one could answer this with 100 percent confidence. Still, you could have made some observations on the general market versus GE. Figure 2.8 is the charted daily S&P 500 price data from May 23, 1999, through August 25, 2000. Note that that the S&P 500 stocks, which are representative of the general market, appear to peak in March 2000.

Figure 2.9 shows the daily GE stock prices for the same time interval.

GE, like the general market, seemed to reach a peak in March 2000, and then there was another August 2000 price jump of GE stock that was not shared by the general market. Since GE's stock price was driven by cost savings rather than by any real product or process innovation, it was unlikely that GE could continue to have such superb results when the rest of the stock market had already peaked. An investor could have used this as a signal to sell GE stock.

As I have stated, I was working at GE while all this was going on. In August 2000, because of the logic I just discussed, I decided to sell most of my GE stock options, even though some of these options had five more years to go before they expired. GE had a way for their management to get cash for their options without actually buying the stock and then selling, and that is what I

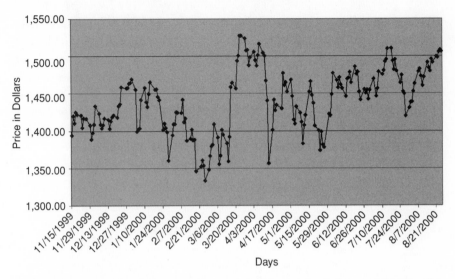

FIGURE 2.8 Daily S&P 500 Stock Prices (Adjusted for Splits and Dividends), 11/15/1999 through 8/25/2000

Source: Data from http://finance.yahoo.com/

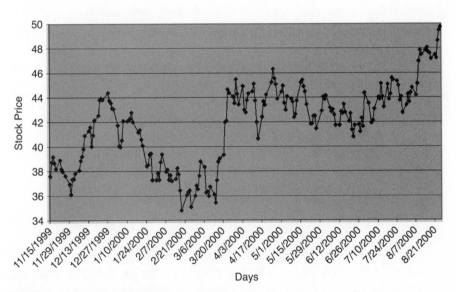

FIGURE 2.9 GE Daily Stock Price (Adjusted for Splits and Dividends), 11/15/1999 through 8/25/2000

Source: Data from http://finance.yahoo.com/

did. However, shortly after putting in my order to cash in my options, I got a call from a GE vice president (so much for privacy). Apparently GE had a trigger that when a manager was selling a large portion of his or her stock options, a vice president was notified. This vice president asked me why I was selling, so I explained my rationale. He said that I was foolish, that GE stock would just keep going up because of GE's superb management and business philosophy. Because of the base price of my stock options, if I had listened to the GE vice president I would have lost 80 percent of my stock options' value! Incidentally, I never got a call back from that vice president acknowledging that I was correct in my decision to sell.

It Is Difficult to Sell a Rising Stock

Despite all my analysis, it was very difficult for me to sell my GE stock options. It is extremely difficult for anyone to sell a stock that has been going up in price for a number of years, no matter what the rationale. It is always tempting to extrapolate your potential future gains and hang on for "just one more year." That is why few investors actually benefited from the huge gain potentials of past time periods when the stock market climbed dramatically. In fact, John Bogle, founder of the very successful Vanguard Group, estimates that the average return for equity funds from 1984 through 2001 was just slightly more than inflation! People just held onto their stocks through the spectacular stock rise of the 1990s and never cashed in! They just rode the stock prices back down.

Key Point

It is extremely difficult for anyone to sell a stock that has been going up in price for a number of years, no matter what the rationale. It is always tempting to extrapolate your potential future gains and hang on for "just one more year."

Whenever a stock is doing well, it is important to periodically review the likelihood of this continuing. There is a bias to hang on to well-performing stocks too long and lose any accumulated gains. Investment analysis helps in that it removes some of the emotion. For example, for most of 2007, I owned stock in a small company called Altair Nanotech, Inc. This company's main product was an innovative battery that had potential in electric cars and for massive power storage in electric utilities. The price of the stock was speculative because the promise of this technology had yet to be realized. The price had gone up substantially since I had purchased it, and I wanted to review whether I should hold it or take my profits and come back another day. One of my concerns was that I thought the overall stock market was dramatically overpriced (as discussed later in the book), but my initial thought was that this stock, being speculative and focused around a product that could help free us from foreign oil, would not be overly affected by a drop in the general stock market. However, I decided to test my "feel" with real data.

Key Point
Whenever a stock is doing well, it is important to periodically review the likelihood of this continuing. There is a bias to hang on to well-performing stocks too long and lose any accumulated gains. Investment analysis helps in that it removes some of the emotion.

I first looked at a 2007 year-to-date graph of the S&P 500 and noted dates of relatively large drops in the S&P 500 value. I found five individual days and one series of several days. I then went into the specific S&P 500 closing prices for those days and calculated the actual percentage price drops. I then went to the Altair Nanotech, Inc., stock price data and looked at Altair stock prices for those days. Table 2.2 shows what I found.

Not only did the Altair stock go down with the general market but also it often went down dramatically more than the market! With Excel, we can calculate probabilities, but this one we can do without Excel! If Altair stock going down was random and not correlated with the S&P 500, we would expect that the chance of the Altair stock price going down being coincident with the S&P 500 price going down would be random, or about half. For Altair to go down the same days as the S&P 500 six times in a row, the random chance would be $\frac{1}{2} \times \frac{1}{2} \times \frac{1}{2} \times \frac{1}{2} \times \frac{1}{2} \times \frac{1}{2} = \frac{1}{64}$, or 1.6 percent. So this correlation between

TABLE 2.2   Large Changes in the S&P 500 versus Altair

Date	S&P 500 Change	Altair Change
2/27/2007	−3.4%	−6.6%
7/23–7/27/2007	−5.3%	−12.8%
8/9/2007	−2.9%	−7.8%
10/19/2007	−2.6%	−4.3%
11/01/2007	−2.6%	−7.8%
11/07/2007	−2.9%	−0.9%

Source: Data from http://finance.yahoo.com

price drops is unlikely to be random, and it looks like a large drop in the S&P 500 is a KPIV for a drop in the Altair stock. Given the sometimes large percentage drops in the Altair stock versus the drops in the S&P 500, a large market drop could be disastrous for shareholders of Altair stock. Because I felt that the whole market was at risk of dropping, I sold my Altair stock.

Did this mean that Altair would then definitely drop in price? Absolutely not! But using data and logic should increase the chance of a correct sell decision rather than just using gut feel or the input of a financial advisor who is likely to be using his or her gut feel. Does this mean that there is a problem with Altair as a company? Again, no! The future for this company may be great. But just like the pizza restaurant, a company can be good but overpriced. Just as the restaurant's growth was in a temporary hold because area development was stymied, I felt that Altair's stock price was at jeopardy because of the high-priced stock market. And if, as I expect, the stock market takes a dramatic drop, I hope to be able to repurchase Altair stock at half of what I sold it for.

When I was discussing my Altair sell decision with a friend, she asked me to see if two restaurant stocks she owned (Chipotle and Tim Horton) would also go down with severe drops in the market. She felt that these two stocks were growing rapidly and could be immune to what I had seen with Altair. So I compared these two stocks with the same market drop dates I had used for Altair. Table 2.3 shows the results.

So, Chipotle restaurant stock went down with the severe S&P 500 drops just as we had seen with Altair. However, the Tim Horton stock seemed to react more independently. When I tried to find out why the two stocks acted differently, I found that the majority of Tim Horton restaurants are in Canada, as is the ownership of the chain, and that is probably the cause of the difference. After seeing this table, my friend asked me what she should do, since she also feared a drop in the U.S. stock market. We agreed that she might be wise to sell Chipotle and buy more Tim Horton, knowing, however, that there was a very real risk that any extended drop in the U.S. markets would eventually affect Canada.

TABLE 2.3   Large Changes in the S&P 500 versus Chipotle and Tim Horton

Date	S&P 500	Chipotle	Tim Horton
2/27/2007	−3.4%	−5.3%	−3.3%
7/23–7/27/2007	−5.3%	−4.9%	−4.4%
8/9/2007	−2.9%	−3.3%	0.2%
10/19/2007	−2.6%	−2.1%	0.7%
11/01/2007	−2.6%	−3.4%	−0.6%
11/07/2007	−2.9%	−0.5%	1.3%

There was one more bit of knowledge I wanted to squeeze out of this study. As mentioned, I feared that the U.S. stock market was about to experience a severe decline. I had been buying two exchange traded funds (ETFs), and I wanted to know how immune they were to the market drops. The first ETF bought Treasury inflation protected securities (TIPS), and the other bought gold. Table 2.4 shows the results for the same S&P 500 drop days.

So, TIPS acted just as I had hoped, and they should be an effective hedge against a severe drop in the stock market. The results from the gold ETF were far more intriguing. Early in the year, gold prices seemed to drop with the general stock market. But recently, gold started to act more independently, and the latest result shows it acting more like TIPS in that it countered the market drop. This is consistent with its general price over the year, where it was flat until September and then rose 30 percent in several months. Gold is a so-called "crisis" investment. It is where investors go when they are worried and confused about the future of the economy and the stock market, which seems to be the current state of affairs. Just as with TIPS, these results on gold bolster my fears that the stock market is getting close to a large drop. Also, it makes me feel comfortable with TIPS, and perhaps gold, as investments of choice for the current economic environment. Of course, readers of this book have the benefit of hindsight to see if this analysis was correct.

The lesson to be learned is that in a severe market drop, most companies' stocks go down with the

Exchange Traded Funds (ETFs)
Funds that track an index but can be traded like a stock

Treasury Inflation Protected Securities (TIPS)
A low-risk, conservative investment that automatically adjusts for inflation, an investment choice that is especially good for anyone who is concerned about high inflation or a possible stock market crash

TABLE 2.4 Large Changes in the S&P 500 versus TIPS and Gold			
Date	S&P 500	TIPs ETF	Gold ETF
2/27/2007	−3.4%	0.9%	−3.9%
7/23–7/27/2007	−5.3%	1.0%	−3.2%
8/9/2007	−2.9%	0.3%	−1.9%
10/19/2007	−2.6%	0.9%	−0.4%
11/01/2007	−2.6%	0.6%	−0.9%
11/07/2007	−2.9%	0.1%	1.0%

market, regardless of the company's individual merits. That is why investors must understand the overall market and economy as well as any individual stock.

Key Point

In a severe market drop, most companies' stocks go down with the market, regardless of the company's individual merits.

Inflation

Before we look at another example, I want to illustrate how inflation distorts the real gains on stocks and why sometimes it is to our benefit to back out the effects of inflation to get a better idea of how our investments are doing. Let's say that you own a share of stock that, including the value of any dividend, keeps a value of $100 per share for three years. Let's also assume that inflation has been running at 3 percent per year. Since the value of the stock has stayed level, its *real* value has *not* kept up with inflation. It has gone down in real value. One of the ways to illustrate this is to adjust the prior years' values to put them in current dollar equivalents. Here's how you do that: The current year's $100 stock value would be worth only 97 percent of its value in the just-prior year if we experienced 3 percent inflation. So, the prior year's value would have been $100/0.97 = $103.09 (in current dollar equivalency). And the stock's value from the year before that would have to be corrected for an additional year of inflation, which would be $103.09/0.97 = $106.28 (in current dollar equivalency). This enables us to look at the relative performance of the stock in a more meaningful way. Inflation hid the fact that the stock was going down in "real" value. In fact, based on the calculations we just did, the equivalent stock performance of a stock in a zero-inflation environment would be that of a stock that was worth $106.28 the first year, $103.09 the second year, and $100 the current year. That is why we often look at stock value in "real" terms to get a more realistic view of its performance.

Key Point

Inflation distorts the real gains on stocks. It is sometimes to our benefit to back out the effects of inflation to get a better idea of how our investments are doing.

Another KPIV for the Stock Market

Everyone is aware that the price of stocks soared in the 1990s. Some people thought it was due to the tech boom or the information advantages brought about by the broad utilization of computers. But there was another possible KPIV that was influencing stock prices. In the 1990s, the percentage of people investing in mutual funds skyrocketed. Much of this growth was the result of 401(k) savings plans. And historically, one of the most consistent drivers of price is demand. Let's see if the demand caused by this increased percentage of ownership correlates visually with the real (without inflation) value of the S&P 500 stocks in the 1990s. Figure 2.10 shows the percentage of households owning mutual funds per year in 1990 through 2002. Figure

Mutual Funds

Combine money from many investors into a fund that actively analyzes and buys stocks, bonds, and other investments

2.11 is the real value of the S&P 500 for the years 1990 through 2000, shown in 2003 dollars and corrected for dividends and stock splits.

The values on Figure 2.10 are generally growing before 1999 and then start to slow and eventually decline. Figure 2.11 peaks in 1999, the same year that the number of households owning mutual funds begins to slow. Note that these charts don't correlate as strongly as the restaurant example charts;

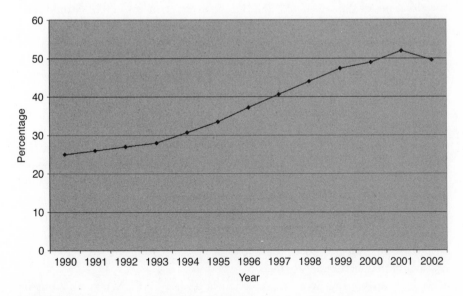

FIGURE 2.10 Percentage of Households Owning Mutual Funds
Source: Data from www.ici.org/pdf/fm-v11n5.pdf

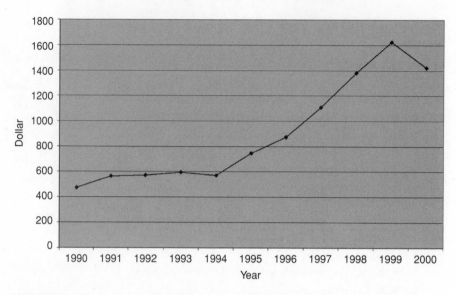

FIGURE 2.11   Real S&P 500 (without Inflation), 2003 Dollar Equivalent

Source: Data from http://finance.yahoo.com/ and www.inflationdata.com/ inflation/Inflation_Rate/HistoricalInflation.aspx

I smoothed the restaurant numbers to illustrate how to use correlations. Nor do I believe that the growing stock ownership was the only KPIV influencing the stock prices during the 1990s. But an investor in early 2000 would have been foolish to ignore data that showed that the demand caused by the growing number of households owning mutual funds peaked in 1999 and that there was some real chance that the growth in stock prices would slow in response. As I am writing this on October 7, 2007, investors are cheering that the S&P 500 price hit 1,557, an all-time high value. After adjusting for inflation, however, the current S&P 500 reading is only 87 percent of the March 24, 2000, S&P 500 reading of 1,527.

Let's go back and look at GE stock with the same type of analysis. We would expect that GE stock prices would also be influenced by the growing demand for stocks in the 1990s, just as we saw for the total S&P 500. However, GE's stock price should also have reflected the fact that earnings in the 1990s were boosted by costs being delayed into future years. Let's see if the inflation-adjusted price for GE stock also shows the price peaking in 2000, but with a strong drop after that peak due to delayed costs and the reduction in the number of people buying stocks.

As I am writing this, GE stock is priced at $41.77. When we compare that with the inflation-adjusted price of GE on August 28, 2000, we see that the current price is only 71 percent of its peak price in the year 2000. That is worse than the overall market, where we just saw that the current price of the S&P 500 is 87 percent of its inflation-adjusted high. So our concern about GE's delayed costs and their influence on GE's profitability after 2000 could indeed have had merit.

Logarithmic Charting

Another tool investors can use is to plot charts logarithmically. This is a custom option in Excel charting. The advantage of logarithmic charting is that it makes a constant percentage yearly increase (or decrease) appear as a sloped straight line. For those interested, how this works is explained in detail in the Appendix. For example, Figure 2.12 gives an initial appearance that the GE stock price is going up at an increasing rate between 1994 and 1999. Figure 2.13 shows the same data plotted logarithmically. Note on the logarithmic plot that for the period between 1994 and 1999 the plot is an upward sloping *straight line*. This says that GE stock was rising at approximately the same percentage rate each of these years. That was not obvious in Figure 2.12.

> **Logarithmic Charting**
> On a logarithmic chart (actually semilog), the vertical axis is spaced equivalent to the power of the plotted number

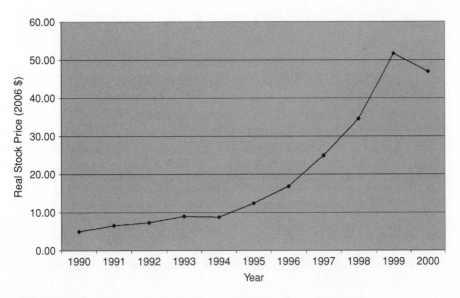

FIGURE 2.12 Real (without Inflation) GE Stock Price (2006 $)

Source: Data from http://finance.yahoo.com/ and www.inflationdata.com/inflation/Inflation_Rate/HistoricalInflation.aspx

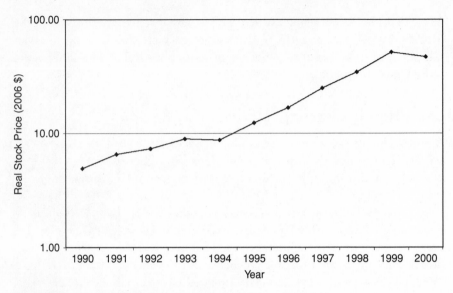

FIGURE 2.13 Logarithmic GE Real Stock Price (2006 $)

Source: Data from http://finance.yahoo.com/ and www.inflationdata.com/inflation/
Inflation_Rate/HistoricalInflation.aspx

Summary

Identifying correlations helps us understand what may be influencing an investment's performance. With this understanding, we can better judge the quality of an investment and its potential.

- Identifying the Key Process Input Variables (KPIVs) affecting an investment is important so you don't get inundated by a multitude of minor details of little importance.

- Charts are a helpful way to see correlations and to spot and analyze KPIVs.

- Correlations can never prove cause and effect. They only give hints, which must then be pursued for further verification.

- It is difficult to sell a rising stock and actually realize a gain because it is so tempting to hold it "just a little longer."

- Inflation can cause a stock price to go up without a "real" improvement in the stock.

Part 2

Quantitative Data Applications

N ow that we have valid data, we can start looking at various visual and quantitative ways of analyzing that data. The chapters in Part 2 give instruction and examples.

Chapter 3: Types of Data

- Variables data
- Proportional data
- Determining variables versus proportional data
- Gauge error

Chapter 4: Probability

- Using Excel to calculate probabilities
- Using Excel's cumulative function
- Random walk, regression, and payout

Chapter 5: Plots and Distributions

- Making a histogram
- Using histograms and line graphs

Chapter 6: Testing Variables Data

- Versus a population
- Versus another sample

Chapter 7: Testing Proportional Data

- Versus a population
- Versus another sample

Chapter 3

Types of Data

There are two types of data, variables and proportional. Variables data, generally given in decimals, are preferred over proportional data, which usually have only two steps or levels. It takes more proportional data than variables data to reach a statistically meaningful conclusion.

Variables and Proportional Data

Variables data (e.g., 3.013, 3.207, 2.998, 3.175), which are usually given as decimals and can have almost infinite resolution, are generally the most valuable type of data. This is because if something is different or changed, you can tell *how much* it has changed, not just whether it changed or not. This enables inferences with fewer data inputs versus proportional data, and it may allow for a higher confidence in the resulting inferences.

> **Variables Data**
> Usually given as decimals and can have almost infinite resolution; generally the most valuable type of data

Proportional data, like qualitative comparisons of more or less, true or false, and higher or lower, often have just two levels of discrimination. This requires much more data to make inferences that have a reasonably high confidence level.

Sometimes it is not obvious whether data are variables or proportional. As a general rule, variables data require at least 10 discriminatory steps. Any data having fewer than 10 possible steps, or levels, should be treated as proportional data.

Proportional Data

Often have just two levels of discrimination, like qualitative comparisons of more or less, true or false, and higher or lower, and more of these data are required to make inferences that have a reasonably high confidence level

To better understand the differences between using variables and proportional data, let's look at an example that also shows the value of removing the effect of inflation from an analysis. From 1973 through 1981, inflation averaged 9.3 percent per year, and most companies' stock prices went up many of these years just because they were riding this wave of inflation.

Figure 3.1 is the graph of the S&P 500 values, adjusted for dividends (dividends included and assumed to be reinvested), for these years.

Table 3.1 shows the S&P 500 values that are used in Figure 3.1.

Looking at these numbers as proportions, we observe that for five of the eight one-year intervals, the S&P 500 went up. However, looking at these data as variables, we can get even more information. For example, we can see that the up years, averaging a 24 percent increase each year, had a much greater average price movement than the down years, which averaged -13 percent. For the total period, the market value, adjusted for dividends, was up 85 percent.

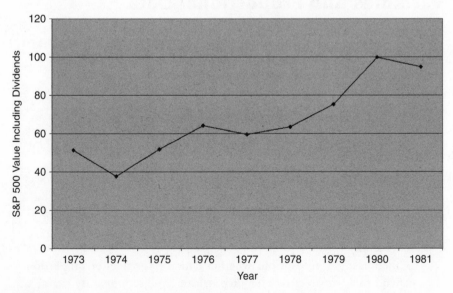

FIGURE 3.1   S&P 500 Including Dividends 1973–1981
Source: Data from http://finance.yahoo.com

TABLE 3.1 Values Used for Figure 3.1	
Dates	S&P 500 Dividend Adjusted
Dec-73	51.3114
Dec-74	37.7306
Dec-75	51.7772
Dec-76	64.1659
Dec-77	59.5739
Dec-78	63.4884
Dec-79	75.3032
Dec-80	99.7795
Dec-81	94.8671

However, when we take out inflation, the story looks quite different. Figure 3.2 is the graph of the same period without inflation.

Table 3.2 shows the data that were used to build Figure 3.2.

Again, looking at these data as proportions, we now observe that for four of the eight one-year intervals, the S&P 500 went up, versus five of the eight years with inflation included. And looking at these data as variables, we can see

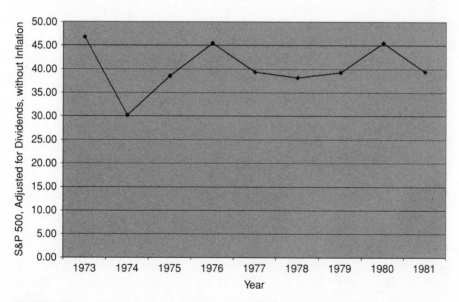

FIGURE 3.2 S&P 500, Years 1973–1981, Adjusted for Dividends, without Inflation

Source: Data from http://finance.yahoo.com and www.inflationdata.com/inflation/ Inflation_Rate/HistoricalInflation.aspx

TABLE 3.2   Values Used for Figure 3.2

Date	S&P 500 Dividend Adjusted, No Inflation
Dec-73	46.84
Dec-74	30.19
Dec-75	38.56
Dec-76	45.46
Dec-77	39.38
Dec-78	38.18
Dec-79	39.27
Dec-80	45.52
Dec-81	39.42

Certificates of Deposit (CDs)

Similar to a savings account at a bank, except that the depositor agrees to keep the money in the account for a specified period of time; CDs pay higher interest rates than savings accounts, but they have a penalty for early withdrawal

that the up years, averaging a 16 percent increase each year, had the same price movement as the down years, which averaged -16 percent. For the total period, the market value, adjusted for dividends, was down 16 percent. (Note that this may seem wrong since the up and down movements were about equal in percentages. But the up periods are always compared to the smaller previous number, and the down periods are always compared to the higher previous number.) This result is radically different than the result with inflation included, which showed a gain of 85 percent.

Now, why is this important? Well, an investor who could have seen the high inflation coming would have looked at other options for investments, such as short term certificates of deposit (CDs), that would have largely kept up with inflation.

If Treasury inflation protected securities (TIPS) had been available then (they weren't, but they are now), which generally pay several percent more than inflation, the gain on owning basically zero-risk TIPS over the same 1973 to 1981 time period would have been 164 percent, versus the 85 percent gain on stocks. This is shown in Figure 3.3. The effects of inflation can fool investors into thinking that their stocks are doing well, whereas other investment options may have performed substantially better!

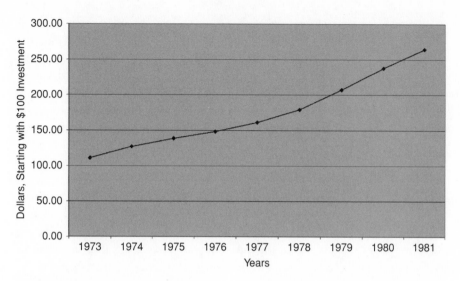

FIGURE 3.3 TIPS (If They Had Been Available) for Years 1973–1981, Starting with a $100 investment

Source: Data from www.inflationdata.com/inflation/Inflation_Rate/HistoricalInflation. aspx

---

Key Point

The effects of inflation can fool investors into thinking that their stocks are doing well, whereas other investment options may have performed substantially better!

Gauge Error

In manufacturing processes, gauge error generally refers to how much of the allowable error (tolerance) is taken-up by errors in the gauge itself. In using data for investing, a similar gauge error issue applies. An investor doesn't want to take action based on changes within the data because of errors in the *method* of collecting the data rather than actual changes in the data caused by real events. For example, unemployment data based on phone interviews may be strongly influenced by the manner in which a question is asked, who answers the phone, the timing of the call (break time?), or even the mood of the person taking the call. Some areas of the

Gauge Error

How much of the allowable error (tolerance) is taken up by errors in the measurement method itself country may be experiencing an economic slowdown or other issues, and the sampling may miss this because the random samples may completely miss the problem areas.

Here is an example. When I was still in college, I manufactured a device to allow quadriplegics to read a book or magazine. This was an extremely low-volume product, and I made it in our home more for satisfaction and to please my wife (who was a nurse taking care of quadriplegics) than for the small amount of profit I realized. One day I received a rather long and detailed questionnaire from the state government regarding my so-called company and this product. They wanted to know all sorts of details about my company, its employees, and its sales. Since on the questionnaire, in small print, it said that filling out the form was voluntary, I ignored it. Some months later, as I was eating dinner, there was a knock on my door. Someone from the state government was there to get the answers to the questionnaire. I explained that the input to the form was voluntary, the amount of my sales was inconsequential, and that I was the only employee. But the questioner was insistent. Since my dinner was getting cold and I couldn't get rid of the person, I finally gave him answers without even going into my financial records to verify the data. He saw that I was generalizing, and he obviously didn't care. We both just wanted to get it over with! If I was typical of the people who gave the government information, I would say that the gauge error related to the questions on that questionnaire was huge!

Key Point

In using data for investing, a similar gauge error issue applies. An investor doesn't want to take action based on changes within the data due to errors in the *method* of collecting the data rather than actual changes in the data caused by real events.

Another possible error is statistical, in that sample size and randomness of data can greatly affect the validity of any conclusions based on the data. The randomness is especially problematic. When election predictions go awry, it generally has nothing to do with the statistics. The major issue is identifying a group of people who are truly representative of the population and polling those people appropriately. To know the makeup and location of this group without already knowing the results of the election is truly problematic.

Key Point

Sample size and randomness of data can greatly affect the validity of any conclusions based on the data.

Solving gauge error is not easy. Even the straightforward gauges used in industry often use more than 30 percent of the allowable tolerance. At the start of an effort at GE to fix gauge error, more than 50 percent of the gauges at GE failed the 30 percent limit. Even after extensive work, 10 percent still failed. And these gauges were more straightforward than what is often needed to measure the economy or the success of a company.

Gauge error is prevalent in much we do. For example, colleges' SATs have long been criticized for having questions that are race and culture sensitive. If that is true, what percentage of the final results is influenced by the inherent error in the SAT test gauge? And grades in different schools and in different parts of the country are not consistent. They are often victims of grade creep or of totally different measurement criteria. Measuring a company's success and potential is equally prone to gauge error.

Summary

Because fewer variables data are required for a valid analysis, they are preferred over proportional data. But no matter which type of data is used for analysis, care must be taken in the method of collecting the data.

- Variables data are usually decimals and can generally have infinite resolution. But as a minimum, variables data must have 10 steps or levels.
- Proportional data are generally based on comparisons, like larger or smaller and true or false. Proportional data require more data than variables data to do a statistically valid analysis.
- Before analyzing data, some thought must be given to the methodology used to gather that data to have confidence that the data are valid.

4

Probability

N othing in life is certain (other than the proverbial death and taxes), and investment success is no exception. Given the uncertainties related to potential investments, we generally want to know the likelihood (probability) of past investment performance being due to just chance variation or to a very specific cause. More important, we want to be able to make some estimate of the probability that the future performance of an investment will be positive. This chapter assists you in calculating and understanding probabilities.

Probability
The likelihood or chance of an event

Using Excel to Calculate Probabilities

Table 4.1 shows the numbers that were used for Figure 2.13, which represents the strong real price growth of GE stock in the 1990s. In fact, if you look at the numbers, in eight of the nine years between 1990 and 1999, the GE stock price went up.

Since these numbers are real and therefore are not influenced by inflation, this is truly a dramatic price performance. Let's look at how unusual this is in comparison with a random change in price, if we assume that a real stock's price would be just as likely to go down as up, which would be a probability of 50 percent, or $p = 0.5$.

Real Price
Comparison of prices without the effect of inflation

TABLE 4.1   GE Real Price Growth in the 1990s

Year	GE without Inflation 2006 $
1990	4.93
1991	6.56
1992	7.33
1993	8.98
1994	8.76
1995	12.38
1996	16.81
1997	24.94
1998	34.60
1999	51.71

Source: Data from http://finance.yahoo.com and www.inflationdata.com/inflation/Inflation_Rate/ HistoricalInflation.aspx

To look at this probability, bring up an Excel worksheet. Click on Insert in the toolbar, and pick Function. A box appears on the screen. Under Category, pick Statistical, and then, under Function, click on BINOMDIST.

In the first box, enter the Number of successes (the number of times the stock price went up), which is 8. The second box asks for the Number of trials (in our example, this is how many years are in our sample), which is 9. The third box asks for the probability of a success (the stock price going up) on each trial, which is 0.5.

The fourth box asks if you want the cumulative probability, which would be the sum of the chances of a stock going up zero times out of nine, going up one time out of nine, two times out of nine, three out of nine . . . all the way up to eight out of nine. We don't want the cumulative probability because all we are interested in is the probability of it going up exactly eight out of nine times. So, we enter False (which means we don't want the cumulative probability). You then get the answer, which is $p = 0.01758$, or less than 2 percent. This is the probability of a stock going up eight out of nine years if its probability of going up or down each year were equal.

We just found the likelihood of the stock going up *exactly* eight out of nine times. However, what we really want to know is the likelihood of a stock going up *at*

Cumulative Probability

The summed probabilities of multiple outcomes

least eight out of nine times. This would also include the likelihood of the stock going up nine out of nine times. You solve for nine out of nine the same way we just did, except the number of successes in the first BINOMDIST box now becomes nine. Solving this, you find that the probability of nine out of nine times is 0.00195. Adding that to the probability of eight out of nine times, we get $0.01758 + 0.00195 = 0.01953$, which still is a probability less than 2 percent.

Using Excel's Cumulative Function

Now, adding the probabilities for eight and nine successes in our example was easy. But what if you wanted to know the probability of a stock randomly going up 40 times in the last 60 trading days, again assuming that the probability of going up on any given day is random, or $p = 0.5$. As we previously stated, what we really want to know is the chance of a stock going up 40 *or more* times out of 60. The chance of hitting one specific number (like 40 in this case) is always low when there are a large number of data points, so hitting *exactly* 40 is not what we are interested in. We *could* calculate the chance of 40 or more in the same way we just did for eight or more out of nine trials, but do we really want to calculate and add together the chances of 40, 41, 42, 43, 44, 45, 46, 47, 48, 49, 50, 51, 52, 53, 54, 55, 56, 57, 58,

> **Cumulative Function**
> A specific function within Excel that sums the probabilities of something happening a given amount of times *or less*

59, and 60 out of 60? That would certainly be possible, but it would also be tedious. Instead, we will use the cumulative function in Excel to calculate this with less fuss.

First, we need one basic logic understanding: The sum of the probabilities of all possible outcomes of an event $= 1$.

For example, the sum of the probabilities of all possible ways to toss a coin, a head or a tail, is $0.5 + 0.5 = 1$. The sum of the probabilities of all possible outcomes of one toss of a die (getting a 1, 2, 3, 4, 5, or 6) are $\frac{1}{6} + \frac{1}{6} + \frac{1}{6} + \frac{1}{6} + \frac{1}{6} + \frac{1}{6} = 1$. We can use this knowledge to use the cumulative function in Excel.

Key Point

The sum of the probabilities of all possible outcomes of an event = 1. We can use this knowledge to use the cumulative function in Excel.

Just to try a simple example, let's redo the earlier problem of eight or more successes in nine trials, assuming that the probability on each trial is 0.5. From our earlier logic statement, if a stock has an equal chance of going up or down on each day, the probability of a stock going up *seven times or less* out of nine times, plus the probability of it going up *eight times or more* out of nine, must be equal to 1! This is because we have included all possible outcomes, and we said that the sum of the probabilities of all possible outcomes of an event $= 1$. So, using simple algebra: 1.0 minus the probability of a stock going up seven times or less out of nine must equal the probability of the stock going up eight times or more out of nine, which is what we desire to know. Since we can use the cumulative function in Excel to find the likelihood of something going up seven or fewer times out of nine, we can then subtract that result from 1 to determine what we want to know: the probability of the stock going up eight or more times out of nine. Let's do this for our example.

Bring up an Excel worksheet. Click on Insert in the toolbar and pick Function. A box appears on the screen. Under Category, pick Statistical, and then, under Function, click on BINOMDIST.

In the first box, enter the Number of successes (the number of times the stock price went up), which is 7. The second box asks for the Number of trials (in our example, this is how many years), which is 9. The third box asks for the probability of a success (the likelihood of the stock price going up) on each trial, which is 0.5. The fourth box asks if you want the cumulative probability, which would be the sum of the chances of a stock going up seven or fewer times out of nine. Since this is what we want, enter True. The probability then comes up: $p = 0.98047$. But as we just discussed, we have to subtract this from 1: $1.0 - 0.98047 = 0.01953$. This $p = 0.01953$ matches the earlier answer we got by adding the probabilities of eight out of nine and nine out of nine.

Let's go back to the earlier example of wanting to know the random chance of a stock going up 40 or more times out of 60 samples. From our earlier logic statement, if a stock has an equal chance of going up or down on each day, or a $p = 0.5$, the probability of a stock going up 39 times or less out of 60 times, plus the probability of it going up 40 times or more out of 60, must be equal to 1! This is because we have included all possible outcomes, and we said that the sum of the probabilities of all possible outcomes of an event $= 1$. So, using simple algebra: 1.0 minus the probability of a stock going up 39 times or less out of 60 must equal the probability of the stock going up 40 times or more out of 60, which is what we desire to know. Since we can use the cumulative function in Excel to find the likelihood of something going up 39 or less times out of 60, we can then subtract that result from 1. Let's do this.

Bring up an Excel worksheet. Click on Insert in the toolbar and pick Function. A box appears on the screen. Under Category, pick Statistical, and then, under Function, click on BINOMDIST.

In the first box, enter the Number of successes (the number of times the stock price goes up), which is 39 (because we want 39 times or less). The second box asks for the Number of trials, which is 60. The third box asks for the probability of a success (the random probability of the stock price going up) on each trial, which is 0.5.

The fourth box asks if you want the cumulative probability, which would be the sum of all the individual probabilities of the stock going up 39 times or fewer times out of 60. Since this is what we want, we type in True. Doing this, we find that the cumulative probability of 39 or less is 0.99326. We need to subtract this from 1 to get the chance of going up 40 or more times out of 60: $1 - 0.99326 = 0.00674$. So, the chance of a stock randomly going up 40 or more times out of 60 times = 0.00674. Note that if you had solved for the probability of a stock going up *exactly 40* out of 60 times, you would have gotten $p = 0.00363$, which is about half the probability you calculated when considering 40 *or more* times.

Random Walk, Regression, and Payout

Per the random walk theory on stocks, at any given time a stock price is just as likely to go up or down. According to this theory, whatever price a stock has at any moment is the best consensus price of all investors, including all the rumors and expectations of the future. Of course, there are many people who have competing thoughts on this, like a regression to the mean tendency of prices. The regression to the mean theory assumes that if a stock, or the stock market in general, is higher priced than it generally was in the past, and there is no known quantitative reason for it to be higher priced, then the price of the stock or stock market is more likely to go down than up. Another way to make some judgment as to whether a stock's price is more likely to go down or up is to value a stock's future payout (dividends) versus what someone can expect to earn on competing investments. If the stock's price is too high versus competing investment opportunities, then the price of the stock is more likely to go down than up.

Random Walk Theory on Stocks
At any given time a stock price is just as likely to go up or down, and whatever price a stock has at any moment is the best consensus price of all investors, including all the rumors and expectations of the future

Regression to the Mean Theory
Assumes that if a stock, or the stock market in general, is higher priced than it generally was in the past, and there is no known quantitative reason that it should be higher priced, then the price of the stock or stock market is more likely to go down than up

Using the random walk assumption that a stock's price has an equal chance of rising or falling, we can look at a stock's recent performance and see how it has done versus a 50 percent probability. If a stock's price has gone up (or down) a statistically significant greater number of times than the 50 percent assumption, than we should consider whether something other than randomness is driving the change in price. However, in apparent violation of the random walk theory, when we look at the stock market in general, specifically the S&P 500, we see that there seems to be a long-term likelihood of the market going up. We can see this in Figure 4.1.

Key Point

If the stock's price is too high versus competing investment opportunities, then the price of the stock is more likely to go down than up.

This chart is shown logarithmically so that uniform changes in data are easier to see. Since the data slopes upward as the years progress, it certainly does not appear that price movement is truly random. There is a tendency for prices to increase over time, not randomly go up and down. Over a period of days or

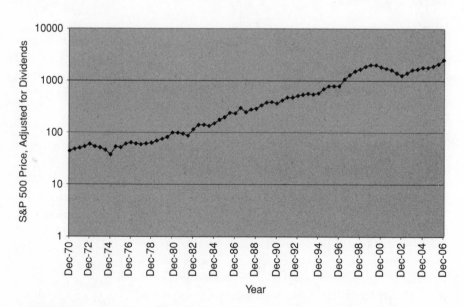

FIGURE 4.1   S&P 500, Adjusted for Dividends, 1970–2006, Six-Month Intervals

Source: Data from http://finance.yahoo.com/

weeks, the probability of an up or down price movement is close to 0.5, but the upward tendency is apparent when longer time periods are examined. This is most likely caused by inflation, but the upward tendency is there no matter what the cause.

Summary

Whenever we evaluate investments, we are making some judgment on probability: the likelihood of the investment increasing in value. So some understanding of probability is needed to do investment analysis.

- Excel can be used to calculate probabilities.
- The random walk theory says that stocks always have an equal chance of going up or down.
- Regression to the mean says that stocks, over time, have a tendency to return to a norm.
- A projected dividend rate can also be used to make a judgment on whether a stock's price is likely to go up or down.

Chapter 5

Plots and Distributions

Much of the information related to stocks or the economy is already plotted on web sites. However, as we have seen, at times you will want to plot data that are *not* already presented in a graph form or plot it in a manner that makes it easier to compare with other data plots. We have already used Excel to generate line charts. Now we will use Excel to generate histograms. You probably already have Microsoft's Excel on your computer, and that is the reason we use Excel's graphing program.

Histogram
A bar graph that is a display of tabulated frequencies

Like line charts, histograms often give insights that are not obvious without the graph. We will use histograms along with line graphs to verify that numerical statistical tests are valid to use for comparisons between multiple sets of data.

Making a Histogram

We will now make a histogram. Copy the 50 sets of numbers shown in Table 5.1 into columns A and B of an Excel worksheet. These are dividend-adjusted prices of the S&P 500 for June 16, 2000, through August 25, 2000.

Recopy the numbers from column B and enter them again into column C. Highlight the numbers in column C, and then order these 50 numbers using the AZ down arrow opposite Sort. If the AZ down arrow is not apparent, go into Data on the toolbar and the AZ arrow will be opposite Sort. Choose Continue with the Current Selection, Sort, and then Ascending. This will order

TABLE 5.1 Dividend-Adjusted Prices for the S&P 500	
Date	S&P 500 Dividend Adjusted 6/16/00–8/25/00
16-Jun-00	1,464.46
19-Jun-00	1,486.00
20-Jun-00	1,475.95
21-Jun-00	1,479.13
22-Jun-00	1,452.18
23-Jun-00	1,441.48
26-Jun-00	1,455.31
27-Jun-00	1,450.55
28-Jun-00	1,454.82
29-Jun-00	1,442.39
30-Jun-00	1,454.60
3-Jul-00	1,469.54
5-Jul-00	1,446.23
6-Jul-00	1,456.67
7-Jul-00	1,478.90
10-Jul-00	1,475.62
11-Jul-00	1,480.88
12-Jul-00	1,492.92
13-Jul-00	1,495.84
14-Jul-00	1,509.98
17-Jul-00	1,510.49
18-Jul-00	1,493.74
19-Jul-00	1,481.96
20-Jul-00	1,495.57
21-Jul-00	1,480.19
24-Jul-00	1,464.29
25-Jul-00	1,474.47
26-Jul-00	1,452.42
27-Jul-00	1,449.62
28-Jul-00	1,419.89
31-Jul-00	1,430.83
1-Aug-00	1,438.10
2-Aug-00	1,438.70

	TABLE 5.1 *(Continued)*
Date	S&P 500 Dividend Adjusted 6/16/00–8/25/00
3-Aug-00	1,452.56
4-Aug-00	1,462.93
7-Aug-00	1,479.32
8-Aug-00	1,482.80
9-Aug-00	1,472.87
10-Aug-00	1,460.25
11-Aug-00	1,471.84
14-Aug-00	1,491.56
15-Aug-00	1,484.43
16-Aug-00	1,479.85
17-Aug-00	1,496.07
18-Aug-00	1,491.72
21-Aug-00	1,499.48
22-Aug-00	1,498.13
23-Aug-00	1,505.97
24-Aug-00	1,508.31
25-Aug-00	1,506.45

the numbers in column C, with the lowest number (1,419.88) at the top and the highest number (1,510.49) at the bottom.

In column D, row 1, enter the formula = (bottom number) − (top number), which in this case will be = C50 − C1, or 1,510.49 − 1,419.88, which is 90.60.

We now want to divide the data into bins. A handy formula for the number of bins is the square root of the number of data points. Since the number of data points is 50, which is close to the number 49, which is 7 squared, the number of bins we will use is 7. (Note that this is only a guideline; it would not be wrong to use 6 or 8 bins, for example.)

In column D, row 2, enter the formula = 1.02*D1/7. This gives us the bin width for 7 bins. The 1.02 in the formula makes the total of all the bin widths slightly wider than the total range of the data. If we wanted a different number of bins, we would change the 7 in the denominator to the desired number of bins. In this case, with 7 bins, the bin width shown in D2 will be 13.20.

Now we have to determine the actual bin edges. In E1, enter the formula = C1-0.01*D1. This will put 1418.98 in E1. This is the left bin edge, which is slightly less than the 1,419.88 minimum data value. In E2, enter the formula

= E1 + \$D\$2. This will cause the next bin edge to be the number in E1 plus the D2 bin width, which will be 1432.19. The \$ signs in the formula cause the bin width to stay the same when we use the formula to determine the remaining bins.

Do Edit, then copy E2. Highlight E3 through E8. (If you had more or fewer bins, you would adjust the number of cells highlighted accordingly.) Click Edit, Paste Special, and then Formulas. This will enter the edge values for the remaining bins. E8 should show the right edge of the last bin, which should be 1511.40. This is slightly more than 1,510.49, which was the highest data number.

For reference, Table 5.2 is what the top 10 lines of the Excel worksheet look like.

In the top header, go to Tools. Click on Data Analysis and then click on Histogram. After the screen appears, highlight column C (your ordered data) and enter it as the Input Range. Click on the second box, Bin Range, and enter the highlighted bin ranges in column E. Choose the options New Worksheet Ply and Chart Output, then click on OK. You will now see the histogram. Drag down the right bottom corner to make the vertical axis longer. The histogram should look similar to the one shown in Figure 5.1.

Normal Distribution
A bell-shaped distribution of data that is indicative of many things in nature including much of the data related to investments

The shape of this distribution is close to a normal distribution, with the majority of the data points in the center of the distribution and fewer data points in the left- and right-hand tails. Real-world data seldom have a perfect normal distribution.

TABLE 5.2   Top Ten Lines of the Excel Worksheet

Date	S&P 500	S&P 500	Widths	Edges
16-Jun-00	1,464.46	1,419.89	90.60	1418.98
19-Jun-00	1,486.00	1,430.83	13.20	1432.19
20-Jun-00	1,475.95	1,438.10		1445.39
21-Jun-00	1,479.13	1,438.70		1458.59
22-Jun-00	1,452.18	1,441.48		1471.79
23-Jun-00	1,441.48	1,442.39		1484.99
26-Jun-00	1,455.31	1,446.23		1498.19
27-Jun-00	1,450.55	1,449.62		1511.40

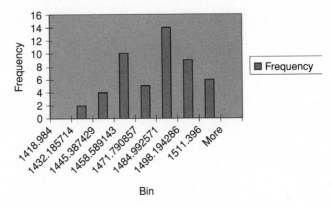

FIGURE 5.1 Histogram

Using Histograms and Line Graphs

When data related to manufacturing samples are examined, those samples are generally taken in a time period short enough that there is no time-related process drift included. Not so in most data on stocks or the economy! Changes over time are very much part of the data composition. That is why we must look at two different types of graphs when trying to decipher the character of the data. We must look at line graphs, which we did earlier in the book, to see any time-related drift. And we must look at histograms to see the data distribution. Here is a simplified example on why we must look at both types of graphs.

Key Point

We must look at two different types of graphs when trying to decipher the character of the data. We must look at line graphs to see any time-related drift, and we must look at histograms to see the data distribution.

Table 5.3 includes two sets of data representing the stock prices of company X for two different time periods. We show the assumed stock prices for 36 days for each sample of data.

Do a histogram for each set of data, using the directions covered in Table 5.3. Figure 5.2 is for the dates January 1 through February 5. Figure 5.3 is for the dates February 29 through April 4.

Although these histograms are not identical, the two periods in which the data were collected gave similarly shaped distributions of data. In order for us to have concluded that the two histograms were different, they would have needed

TABLE 5.3 Stock Prices of Company X for Two Time Periods

Company X

Time Period 1		Time Period 2	
Day	Price	Day	Price
1/1	84	2/29	138
1/2	85	3/1	138
1/3	83	3/2	136
1/4	87	3/3	135
1/5	88	3/4	134
1/6	89	3/5	133
1/7	89	3/6	134
1/8	91	3/7	131
1/9	92	3/8	130
1/10	93	3/9	129
1/11	94	3/10	126
1/12	92	3/11	126
1/13	96	3/12	126
1/14	97	3/13	125
1/15	99	3/14	124
1/16	99	3/15	123
1/17	100	3/16	122
1/18	100	3/17	127
1/19	99	3/18	122
1/20	100	3/19	122
1/21	101	3/20	121
1/22	102	3/21	117
1/23	105	3/22	120
1/24	107	3/23	118
1/25	105	3/24	117
1/26	103	3/25	116
1/27	107	3/26	120
1/28	111	3/27	114
1/29	109	3/28	105
1/30	111	3/29	120
1/31	111	3/30	111
2/1	112	3/31	112
2/2	112	4/1	111
2/3	112	4/2	107
2/4	117	4/3	107
2/5	116	4/4	106

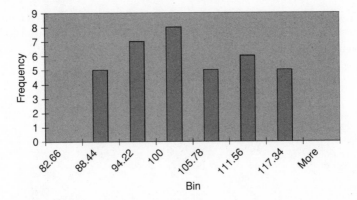

FIGURE 5.2 Histogram for Company X, January
1 through February 5

totally different shapes, like one of the two histograms having most of the data
in the left bins and the other histogram having the majority of the data in the
right bins.

Key Point

In order for us to have concluded that the two histograms were different,
they would have needed totally different shapes, like one of the two
histograms having most of the data in the left bins and the other
histogram having the majority of the data in the right bins.

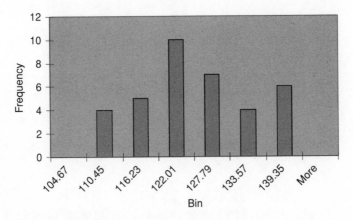

FIGURE 5.3 Histogram for Company X, February 29
through April 4

As we said, we must also look at these data using the line charts to see if during one collection period the data were coming in a substantially different order than in the other data period. Figure 5.4 is for dates January 1 through February 5. Figure 5.5 is for dates February 29 through April 4.

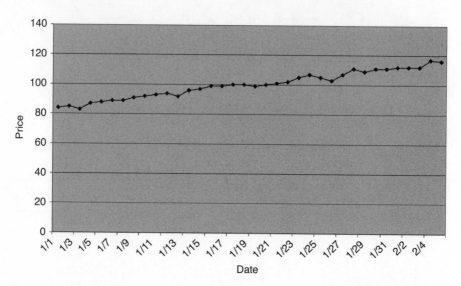

FIGURE 5.4   Company X Stock Price January 1 through February 5

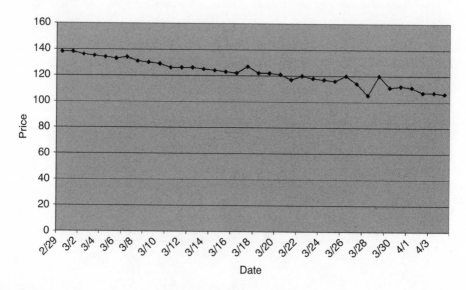

FIGURE 5.5   Company X Stock Price February 29 through April 4

Note that the slopes of the two graphs, Figures 5.4 and 5.5, are opposite each other. During the Figure 5.4 data period, the price of Company X stock was rising. In Figure 5.5, the price was falling. The issue is *not* that the prices in Figure 5.5 are generally higher. If that were the only difference, the slopes of the lines would be similar, just higher on one graph. But in this case, the total personalities of the two periods are different, with the one having rising prices and the other having dropping prices. This precludes us from doing numerical statistical tests on the data, which would be comparing apples and oranges. Two apples can be different in size or in different positions and still be compared as two apples. But when two graphs have totally different shapes like these, the two periods of stock price collection are not equivalent. This is often an important finding, and the reasons for the differences may be worth pursuing.

Key Point

When two graphs have totally different shapes, the two periods of stock price collection are not equivalent.

Next we need to cover some statistical tests for instances where the basic shapes of the graphs are *not* dissimilar.

Summary

To do numerical statistical tests, we must first be sure that the data we are comparing are similar so that we are not comparing apples and oranges. This is especially true for evaluating investments whose character may change dramatically over time. We must use charts or graphs to visually examine the data before we do numerical tests.

- Line graphs are used to see any time-related drift.
- Histograms are used to determine if the data distribution stays reasonably the same.

Chapter

6

Testing Variables Data

ariables data are generally in decimal form with many possible data
steps. Samples of these data can be compared with population data
(a large number of previous data points over an extended period of time)
or with other stocks having similar data characteristics.

In this chapter, GE is our example for testing variables data. Using what
we learned from the previous chapter, we first use charts to make sure that the
data are similar in nature. We then compare the numerical variation within
each set of data, testing for differences that are statistically significant. Last, we
compare the numerical averages of each set of data, again testing for statistical
differences.

The Three Steps of Comparing Variables Data

To compare two sets of variables data to see if there is a statistically significant
difference between the two, we do three steps. First, we plot the data to see if
the plot shapes are significantly different. We need to examine plots of the data
distribution, which we did with the histograms and line graphs in the previous
chapter. If either of these plotting methods shows a substantial shape change,
then that is enough for us to know that there is a significant difference. If the
plot shapes are not significantly different, we can then do numerical statistical
checks comparing the variation within each data set. Just as with the plots, if
there are significant differences in the variations of the data, this is often worth

noting. And last, if the earlier two tests of distribution or variation do not show significant differences, we can then compare the averages of the two groups to see if they are statistically different.

Key Point

If the two tests of distribution or variation do not show significant differences, we can then compare the averages of the two groups to see if they are statistically different.

Looking for significant differences in this way often saves us the time of detailed examination of differences that are trivial and not statistically significant. When the data show significant differences, this finding can trigger us to look further at a change that may be important and valuable to us in looking at investment opportunities.

Let's go back and take another look at a graph we used in Chapter 2. We will relabel it as Figure 6.1.

Visually, it appears that we have three discrete different values for the six-month average interval differences for GE minus the S&P 500. For the 49 values up to June 1998, the average is 0.0206. For the 7 values between July 1998 and June 2001, the average is 0.0752. And for the 11 values after June 2001,

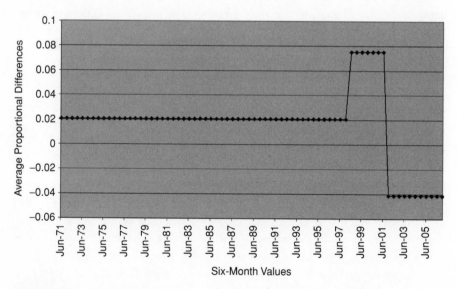

FIGURE 6.1 Six-Month Interval Average Differences: GE Minus S&P 500, June 1971–June 1998, July 1998–June 2001, July 2001–December 2006
Source: Data from http://finance.yahoo.com/

the average is -0.0414. To improve our confidence that these differences are *not* random and are indeed likely to have been caused by some real change, we must do some statistical checks on the data.

Key Point

To improve our confidence that these differences are *not* random and are indeed likely to have been caused by some real change, we must do some statistical checks on the data.

Checking the Graphs or Charts

The first check is to graphically chart each set of numbers and see if the shapes of the distributions are similar. Note that I said similar, not identical! We are only concerned when there are large enough differences between the shapes of the graphs that would make us confident that the process, or in this case the nature of the stock prices or the overall market, has totally changed in nature. If we see a large change in the overall shape of the plotted data, we assume that the underlying personality of the stock prices or the total market has changed. Then the statistical tests that we want to do will no longer be valid or required. However, the discovery of such a difference is often invaluable because it would make an investor cognizant that an important market change may have occurred, perhaps in the transition from a positive bull market to a negative bear market.

Key Point

The discovery of a large difference in the overall shape of plotted data is often invaluable because it would make an investor cognizant that an important market change may have occurred, perhaps in the transition from a positive bull market to a negative bear market.

First, let's look at the line charts of the flow data from each of the three levels that are shown in Figure 6.1. Figure 6.2 is the June 1971 through June 1998 interval proportional differences between GE price changes minus the S&P 500 price changes. Figure 6.3 shows the interval proportional differences between GE price changes minus the S&P 500 price changes for July 1998 through June 2001. And Figure 6.4 shows the interval proportional differences between GE price changes minus the S&P 500 price changes for July 2001 through December 2006.

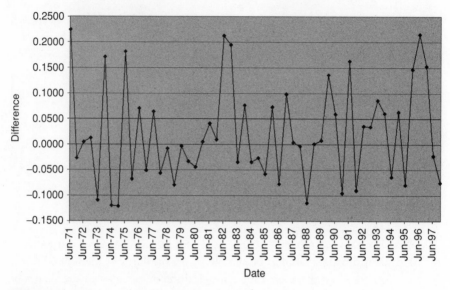

FIGURE 6.2   GE versus S&P 500, June 1971–June 1998
Source: Data from http://finance.yahoo.com/

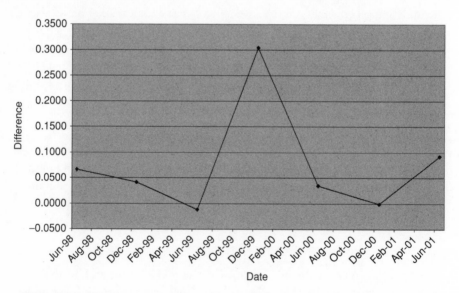

FIGURE 6.3   GE versus S&P 500, July 1998–June 2001
Source: Data from http://finance.yahoo.com/

There are no radical differences between these charts; they are similar in shape. Granted, with the limited data included in Figure 6.3, this determination is difficult. But with these data, we can't conclude any substantial differences.

Now let's look at the histograms showing the data distributions for each of the three time intervals. Figure 6.5 is the June 1971 through June 1993

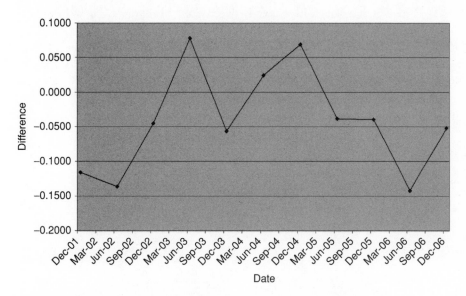

FIGURE 6.4 GE versus S&P 500, July 2001–December 2006
Source: Data from http://finance.yahoo.com/

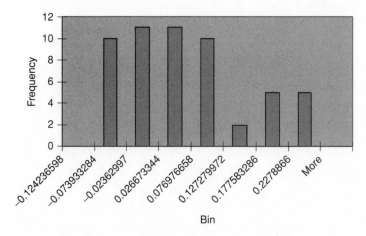

FIGURE 6.5 GE Minus S&P 500 Differences, June
1971–June 1998
Source: Data from http://finance.yahoo.com/

interval proportional differences between GE price changes minus the S&P 500 price changes. Figure 6.6 shows the interval proportional differences between GE price changes minus the S&P 500 price changes for July 1998 through June 2001. And Figure 6.7 shows the interval proportional differences between GE price changes minus the S&P 500 price changes for July 2001 through December 2006.

There are no huge differences between these histograms. They show similar distributions of data, with the frequency slightly skewed to the left-hand side of the histogram. Again, with the limited data included in Figure 6.6, it is difficult to be sure of the shape. But with the limited data (which is often a real-world limitation), we can't conclude substantial differences. So we can proceed with the numerical statistical tests of the data.

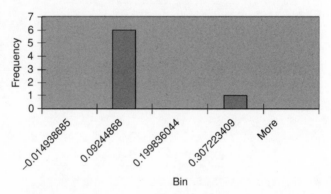

FIGURE 6.6   GE Minus S&P 500 Differences, July 1998–June 2001

Source: Data from http://finance.yahoo.com/

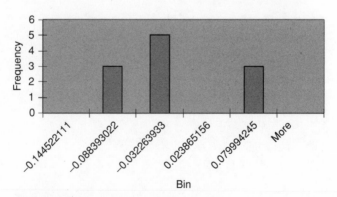

FIGURE 6.7   GE Minus S&P 500 Differences, July 2001–December 2006

Source: Data from http://finance.yahoo.com/

Comparing a Population to a Data Sample

We want to compare different data groups statistically. There are two different types of data groups we can compare. We can compare a population (requires at least 30 data points) to a data sample, or we can compare two samples of data with each other. In our previous example, there were 54 data points included in the time period of June 1971 through June 1998. Since that is more than 30 data points, we can consider this as a population. So, for our first example, let's compare the third group of data (July 2001 through December 2006), which has 11 data points, to the population of the first group.

Key Point

There are two different types of data groups we can compare. We can compare a population (requires at least 30 data points) to a data sample, or we can compare two samples of data with each other.

To do this, I listed the data of each group in an Excel worksheet. Then, in a cell below the population data, I entered an = sign. I went into Insert in the Header Bar, then Function, then AVERAGE, and OK. I then got a Functions Argument box. I clicked on Number 1 box and deleted any numbers already in the box. Then I highlighted the population data. I clicked on OK in the Functions Argument box. In the cell below the population data, I could now see the average, which in this case was 0.0206.

In a cell below the average value just found, I entered an = sign. I then went into Insert in the Header Bar, then Function, then STDEV, and OK. I then got a Functions Argument box and clicked on Number 1 box. I deleted any numbers already in the box and then highlighted the population data. I clicked on OK in the Functions Argument box. In the cell below the average value, I then saw the standard deviation (sigma), which in this case is 0.09542. The standard deviation, or sigma, of a group of numbers is a measure of the variation of values within those numbers. The more uniform and consistent the numbers, the lower the sigma will be. The more variation within the data, the larger the sigma will be. A statistics textbook provides a more detailed definition of sigma or standard deviation, but this is all the definition we need for the work we will be doing.

Standard Deviation (or Sigma)

A measure of the variation of values within a group of numbers: the more uniform and consistent the numbers, the lower the sigma, and the more variation within the group of numbers, the larger the sigma

I then did the same thing for the data column representing our 11 data point sample from July 2001 through December 2006. Following the previous directions, I found that the sample average is -0.0414 and the sample sigma is 0.07469.

The symbol we will use for sample average is $\bar{x}$, and the symbol for the population average will be $\bar{X}$. The symbol for the sample sigma will be s, whereas the symbol for the population sigma will be S. Some statistics books use Greek letters, but $\bar{x}$, $\bar{X}$, s, and S are perfectly acceptable.

Comparing the Variations (Sigmas)

Chi-Square Test

A test done to check a population's sigma against a sample's sigma

We will first see if the sigmas of each of the two groups are significantly different. If they are, it would mean that the variation of data within one group is far different than the variation of data within the other group, and therefore no more tests are required to say that the two groups of data are significantly different. To check a population's sigma against a sample's sigma, we do a chi-square test (rhymes with guy-square). Note that to get a valid sigma on a sample, we need a minimum sample size of 11 data points, which it just so happens we have.

Here is the formula for the chi-square test value:

$$\text{Chi}_{t^2} = \frac{(n-1)s^2}{S^2} \qquad (6.1)$$

So let's calculate the chi-square test value for our sample.

$$\text{Chi}_{t^2} = \frac{(n-1)s^2}{S^2} = \frac{(11-1)0.07469^2}{0.09542^2} = 6.13 \qquad (6.2)$$

Now that we have the chi-square test value, we have to test it! We will do that by looking in Table 6.1 to see if the calculated test value is higher or lower than the numbers that apply to the sample size of $n = 11$. If the calculated chi-square test value of 6.13 falls outside the acceptable range (higher than the high table number or lower than the low table number), then we will conclude that the sigmas of the population and the sample are different, to a confidence level of 95 percent.

Comparing our calculated chi-square test value of 6.13 with the values in the $n = 11$ row of the table, we see that 6.13 is not lower than 3.25 or higher than 20.48, so we can *not* be 95 percent confident that the sigmas are different.

TABLE 6.1   Chi-Square Distribution Table to Test
a Sample Sigma *s* (with Sample Size *n*) versus a
Population Sigma *S*

n	Low	High
11	3.25	20.48
12	3.82	21.92
13	4.4	23.34
14	5.01	24.74
15	5.63	26.12
16	6.26	27.49
17	6.91	28.85
18	7.56	30.19
19	8.23	31.53
20	8.91	32.85
21	9.59	34.17
22	10.28	35.48
23	10.98	36.78
24	11.69	38.08
25	12.4	39.36
26	13.12	40.65
27	13.84	41.92
28	14.57	43.19
29	15.31	44.46
30	16.05	45.72
31	16.79	46.98
32	17.54	48.23
33	18.29	49.48
34	19.05	50.73
35	19.81	51.97
40	23.65	58.12
45	27.57	64.2
50	31.55	70.22

(continued on next page)

	TABLE 6.1 (*Continued*)	
n	*Low*	*High*
55	35.59	76.19
60	39.66	82.12
70	47.92	93.86
80	56.31	105.47
90	64.79	116.99
100	73.36	128.42

95% confident the sigmas are different if Chi $_{t^2}$ is less than the table low number or higher than the table high number

So we can move on to the next step and check for significant differences in the averages.

Comparing the Averages

t Test
Checks for a statistically significant change in variables data averages when comparing a sample and a population or two samples

We will now compare the June 1971 through June 1998 population average $\overline{X}$ to the July 2001 through December 2006 sample average $\overline{x}$. To do this we must calculate a t test value (t_t).

Following is the formula for the t test of a population average $\overline{X}$ versus a sample average $\overline{x}$:

t test of a population average $\overline{X}$ versus a sample average $\overline{x}$ with a sample size n

$$t_t = \frac{|\overline{x} - \overline{X}|}{\frac{s}{\sqrt{n}}} \qquad (6.3)$$

$$t_t = \frac{|-0.0414 - 0.0206|}{\frac{0.07469}{\sqrt{11}}} = 2.75 \qquad (6.4)$$

Note that, in the formula, the difference between the averages is an absolute number, so ignore any minus sign in the difference.

Now that we have the t test value, we have to test it! We will do that by looking in the distribution table (Table 6.2) to see if the calculated t test value of 2.75 is higher than the t value that applies to the sample size of $n = 11$. If it *is* higher, then we can be 95 percent confident that the population average $\overline{X}$ is different than the sample average $\overline{x}$.

Since the calculated t test value of 2.75 is higher than the table t value of 2.23 that applies to the sample size of $n = 11$, we can conclude, with a 95 percent level of confidence, that the June 1971 through June 1998 population average $\overline{X}$ of the intervals of GE stock prices minus the S&P 500 prices are different than the July 2001 through December 2006 sample average $\overline{x}$ of the intervals of GE stock prices minus the S&P 500 prices. This tends to support our suspicion that the delayed GE costs of the late 1990s did indeed cause the later GE stock prices to be lower than the comparable S&P 500 stock prices.

TABLE 6.2   t Distribution Table

To Compare a Sample Average (size = n) to a Population Average; or to Compare Two Samples of Sizes n_1 and n_2 Using $n = (n_1 + n_2 - 1)$

n	t value
6	2.57
7	2.45
8	2.37
9	2.31
10	2.26
11	2.23
12	2.2
13	2.18
14	2.16
15	2.15
16	2.13
17	2.12
18	2.11
19	2.1
20	2.09

(continued on next page)

TABLE 6.2 (Continued)	
n	t value
21	2.09
22	2.08
23	2.07
24	2.07
25	2.06
30	2.05
35	2.03
40	2.02
50	2.01
60	2
80	1.99
100+	1.98

If the calculated t_t test value exceeds the table t value, then the two averages being compared are significantly different to a 95 percent confidence.

Comparing Another Population to a Data Sample

We never did numerical checks related to the middle July 1998 through June 2001 group of data. And the reason we did not do that comparison is because the seven data points in this grouping are not sufficient for us to determine a valid sigma. Since this middle level of data is important for us to understand the full story of the GE stock price going up and then down versus the general market, I had to go back and get the required additional data! This middle level of data is what influenced my decision to sell my GE stock options. The last group of data only validated my decision, as least as far as what happened to GE stock prices.

Since the prior stock intervals were six months, I had to get data for shorter time intervals to get the required sample size. Revisiting intervals because of sample size requirements is not unusual. Often, when doing numerical analysis, you see a time period of interest but find that you need more data to do a valid statistical analysis. That is what I had to do now. I got 11 data points, the same number of data points as in our other sample. Similar sample sizes are preferred when comparing two samples. For this example, I obviously could have shown the additional samples up front; but I wanted to emphasize that someone should not hesitate to go back for additional samples once time periods of interest are identified.

Once I obtained the required 11 data points for the July 1998 through June 2001 period, I calculated the related average $\bar{x} = 0.0752$ and a sigma $s = 0.0806$ for that data. I also revalidated that the shape of the distributions being compared were not significantly different.

Comparing the Variations (Sigmas)

We now want to compare this July 1998 through June 2001 sample to the first June 1971 through June 1998 population group, just as we did with the previous sample. We first check to see if the sigmas of the two groups are significantly different. If they are, it means that the variation of data within one group is far different than the variation of data within the other group, and therefore no more tests are required to say that the population and the sample are significantly different. To check the population's sigma against the sample's sigma, we have to do a chi-square test.

Again, here is the formula for the chi-square test value:

$$\text{Chi}_{t^2} = \frac{(n-1)s^2}{S^2} \tag{6.5}$$

Calculating the chi-square test value for our sample:

$$\text{Chi}_{t^2} = \frac{(n-1)s^2}{S^2} = \frac{(11-1)0.0806^2}{0.09542^2} = 7.13 \tag{6.6}$$

Now that we have the chi-square test value, we have to test it! We will do that by looking in the previous chi-square table (Table 6.1) to see if the calculated test value is higher or lower than the numbers that apply to the sample size of $n = 11$. If the calculated chi-square test value of 7.13 falls outside the acceptable range (higher than the high table number or lower than the low table number), then we would conclude that the sigmas of the population and the sample are different (to a confidence level of 95 percent).

Comparing our calculated chi-square test value of 7.13 with the values in the $n = 11$ row of Table 6.1, we see that 7.13 is not lower than 3.25 or higher than

Acceptable Range

Not higher than the high chi-square table number or lower than the low chi-square table number

20.48, so we can *not* be 95 percent confident that the sigmas are different. So, we can move on to the next step and check for significant differences in the averages.

Comparing the Averages

That means that we can now compare the June 1971 through June 1998 population average $\overline{X}$ to the July 1998 through June 2001 sample average $\overline{x}$. To do this we must calculate a *t* test value (t_t). Again, here is the formula for the *t* test of a population average $\overline{X}$ versus a sample average $\overline{x}$:

t test of a population average $\overline{X}$ versus a sample average $\overline{x}$ with a sample size n

$$t_t = \frac{|\overline{x} - \overline{X}|}{\dfrac{s}{\sqrt{n}}} \tag{6.7}$$

$$t_t = \frac{|0.0752 - 0.0206|}{\dfrac{0.0806}{\sqrt{11}}} = 2.25 \tag{6.8}$$

Now that we have the *t* test value, we have to test it! We do that by looking in the previous *t* distribution table (Table 6.2), and we see that the calculated *t* test value of 2.25 is higher than the 2.23 table *t* value that applies to the sample size of $n = 11$. Since it *is* higher, then we can be 95 percent confident that the sample average $\overline{x}$ is different than the population average $\overline{X}$. This supports our observation that the rise in GE stock prices versus the S&P 500 in the 1998 through 2001 period compared with the 1971 through 1998 period was probably real and not the result of random price changes.

Comparing Two Data Samples

F Test
Checks for a statistically significant change in variables data sigmas when comparing two samples

We will do one more numerical check, which is the July 1998 through June 2001 sample (the middle group of data) versus the July 2001 through December 2006 (the third group of data).

Comparing the Variations (Sigmas)

To compare the sigmas between two samples of a similar size n, we do an *F* test. Here is the formula.

F test comparing two sample sigmas

$$F_t = \frac{s_1^2}{s_2^2}$$ (6.9)

s_1 = sample with the larger sigma
s_2 = sample with the smaller sigma

The sample sizes n should be within 20 percent of each other.
Let's calculate this F test for our two samples.

$$F_t = \frac{s_1^2}{s_2^2} = \frac{0.0806^2}{0.0747^2} = 1.164$$ (6.10)

We now have to test this result to see if we can make any conclusions about the sigmas.

Since the F test calculation of 1.164 does not exceed the Table 6.3 F table test value of 2.98, we can *not* assume, with 95 percent confidence, that the two sample sigmas are significantly different. So, we can move on to the next step and check for significant differences in the averages.

TABLE 6.3   F Table for Comparing Sigmas from Two Samples (Sizes = n_1 and n_2)

N	F
11	2.98
12	2.82
13	2.69
14	2.58
15	2.48
16	2.4
17	2.33
18	2.27
19	2.22
20	2.17
21	2.12
22	2.08
23	2.05
24	2.01
25	1.98
26	1.96
27	1.93
28	1.9

(continued on next page)

TABLE 6.3 (*Continued*)	
N	F
29	1.88
30	1.86
31	1.84
32	1.82
33	1.8
34	1.79
35	1.77
36	1.76
37	1.74
38	1.73
39	1.72
40	1.7
42	1.68
44	1.66
46	1.64
48	1.62
50	1.61
60	1.54
70	1.49
80	1.45
100	1.39
120	1.35
150	1.31
200	1.26
300	1.21
400	1.18
500	1.16
750	1.13
1000	1.11

At 95 percent confidence (sample sizes should be equal within 20 percent)

$$\text{Table } N = \frac{n_1 + n_2}{2}$$

If the calculated F_t value exceeds the table value F, assume a significant difference between the sigmas.

Comparing the Averages

We will proceed in testing to see if the two sample averages are significantly different. For this, we will use a t test for two sample averages.

t test of two sample averages $\bar{x}_1$ and $\bar{x}_2$

$$t_t = \frac{|\bar{x}_1 - \bar{x}_2|}{\sqrt{\left(\dfrac{n_1 s_1^2 + n_2 s_2^2}{n_1 + n_2}\right)\left(\dfrac{1}{n_1} + \dfrac{1}{n_2}\right)}} \qquad (6.11)$$

$\bar{x}_1$ and $\bar{x}_2$ are two samples averages
s_1 and s_2 are the sigmas on the two samples
n_1 and n_2 are the two sample sizes
$|\bar{x}_1 - \bar{x}_2|$ is the absolute difference between the averages, ignoring a minus sign in the difference.

$$t_t = \frac{|\bar{x}_1 - \bar{x}_2|}{\sqrt{\left(\dfrac{n_1 s_1^2 + n_2 s_2^2}{n_1 + n_2}\right)\left(\dfrac{1}{n_1} + \dfrac{1}{n_2}\right)}} \qquad (6.12)$$

$$t_t = \frac{|0.0414 - 0.0752|}{\sqrt{\left(\dfrac{11(0.07469)^2 + 11(0.0806)^2}{11 + 11}\right)\left(\dfrac{1}{11} + \dfrac{1}{11}\right)}} = 1.02 \quad (6.13)$$

Now that we have the t test value, we have to test it! We will do that by looking in the previous t distribution table (Table 6.2) to see if the calculated t test value of 1.02 is higher than the t value that applies to the sample size of $n = 11$ for each sample (we use $n = 21$ for the table). If it *is* higher, then we can be 95 percent confident that the two sample averages are different.

Since the calculated t test value of 1.02 is *not* higher than the table t value of 2.09 that applies to the table adjusted sample size of $n = 21$, we can *not* conclude, with a 95 percent confidence, that the July 1998 through June 2001 sample average $\bar{x}$ of the intervals of GE stock prices minus the S&P 500 prices are different than the July 2001 through December 2006 sample average $\bar{x}$ of the intervals of GE stock prices minus the S&P 500 prices. The reason that we cannot conclude this difference relates to the fact that the sample sizes of 11 on each sample are small, so the confidence of the sigma on each sample is minimal. That makes the t test very difficult to pass. Again, we have to go back and get more data if we want to see if there is a real probable difference. And indeed, although I don't show the detail here, when a larger sample is used, the difference between the two samples is significant. Sample size n is your friend, and sometimes you need many friends!

Actual Use of These Tests

When I got close to selling my GE stock options, I went to sample frequencies far greater than those shown in the GE statistics example. I set up the same equations, GE stock prices, and the S&P 500 prices in a spreadsheet on my computer. Then every evening I updated the data with that day's results. I used the most recent 15 days for the sample and the most recent 50 trade days just prior to the 15 recent days as the reference population. I just entered the current day's results, and the computer calculated all the formulas and compared the results to the test values. Note that this is not without issue, because every two weeks, on the average, I would get an alarm related to a formula's calculations that were outside the test values specified in the various tables. This kind of alarm is expected in that all the statistics that were used are based on a 95 percent confidence level. That means that 5 percent of the time I would get an alarm on either the sigma or the average, and then I would have to investigate further. You can set up statistical tests to respond at a higher confidence level so you get fewer alarms, but then the tests may be so insensitive that you miss an opportunity to take timely action. Also, higher confidence levels are generally not justified, given all the other inaccuracies involved with input data. No matter what, other information and judgment, in addition to quantitative analysis, have to be used in any decision related to investments, so greater accuracy on the data analysis is not appropriate in most cases.

Key Point

No matter what numerical result is found, other information and judgment, in addition to quantitative analysis, have to be used in any decision related to investments. Greater accuracy on the data analysis is not appropriate in most cases.

You can also set up statistical tests that respond to a lower confidence level. But then you will get a proportionally larger number of alarms. A 95 percent confidence level seems to be about the right amount of sensitivity for looking for a statistically significant change.

Summary

Although statistical tests of variables data may seem formidable, walking through the steps shown in this chapter will enable anyone to use these powerful tools. Statistical testing gives a sizable advantage to investors who can do them.

- First, use graphs or charts to make sure that the data is appropriate for numerical testing.
- Then, test for significant differences between the variations (sigmas).
- If there is no significant difference in the sigmas, test for significant differences between the averages.

Testing Proportional Data

Proportional data are based on attributes, like good-bad, yes-no, greater-lesser, and increasing-decreasing. They are often given as ratios, like the proportion of increasing stock prices versus decreasing prices in a given number of days. Even if the results are shown as decimals, however, they can *not* be treated as variables data unless they have at least 10 possible data step values within the period of study.

> **Population Data**
>
> A large number of data points over an extended period of time

Samples of proportional data can be compared with the population or with other sets of similar sample data. However, much more data will be required to see a statistical change when using proportional data than the sample sizes required with variables data.

In this chapter, the price change of a stock for a period of time illustrates the use of statistical tests on proportional data.

Comparing a Stock Price Change Proportion of a Sample to a Recent Population's Stock Price Change

As a way to learn how to test proportional data, we want to compare sample results showing the proportional number of times a stock price rose compared with recent historical data. We will compare a sample's proportional results p to historical proportional results P, with any difference indicated at a 95 percent confidence level.

Key Point

As a way to learn how to test proportional data, we want to compare sample results showing the proportional number of times a stock price rose compared with recent historical data.

Here is the test ratio:

Test ratio for comparing a proportional sample with the population (95 percent confidence)

$$\text{Sample/Population Test Ratio} = \frac{|p - P|}{\sqrt{\dfrac{P(1 - P)}{n}}}$$

P = proportion in the population
p = proportion in the sample
$|p - P|$ = absolute proportion difference (no minus sign in difference)
n = size of sample

If the test ratio result is greater than 2, then we can say with 95 percent confidence that the sample proportion is statistically different than the population proportion.

Let's try this on an example. Assume that we have data on 550 recent hourly up-or-down readings on a stock's price. Assume that the number of up readings on this sample was 245, for a $p = 245/550$ or $p = 0.445$. We know that historically the up readings of the population of this stock's price have been 49.1 percent, or $P = 0.491$.

Key Point

If the test ratio result is greater than 2, then we can say with 95 percent confidence that the sample proportion is statistically different than the population proportion.

We would like to know if the recent lower proportion of up readings is significant such that we should be concerned that something about the stock is causing it to drop in price versus its historical performance.

$$\text{Sample/Population Test Ratio} = \frac{|p - P|}{\sqrt{\dfrac{P(1 - P)}{n}}} = \frac{|0.445 - 0491|}{\sqrt{\dfrac{0.491(1 - 0.491)}{550}}} = 2.158$$

Since 2.158 is greater than 2, we can assume, with 95 percent confidence, that the sample having 44.5 percent up readings has a statistically significantly lower number of up readings than the 49.1 percent up readings of the historical population. That means that we would be 95 percent confident that the sample was truly different than the population, and we should be concerned about its recent price performance.

Comparing Two Data Samples

We can also compare two proportional data samples. Let's continue with the previous example and assume that some time later we have data on a larger sample, this one with a sample size of $n = 650$. This new sample has 314 up readings. We would like to know if the two samples are statistically different as to the percentage of up readings.

First, here is the sample/sample test ratio we will calculate to see if these two samples are significantly different.

Comparing two proportional data samples

$$\text{Sample/Sample Test Ratio} = \frac{\left| \dfrac{x_1}{n_1} - \dfrac{x_2}{n_2} \right|}{\sqrt{\left(\dfrac{x_1 + x_2}{n_1 + n_2} \right)\left(1 - \dfrac{x_1 + x_2}{n_1 + n_2} \right)\left(\dfrac{1}{n_1} + \dfrac{1}{n_2} \right)}}$$

$x_1 = $ number of up readings (or whatever is being counted) in sample #1

$x_2 = $ number of up readings (or whatever is being counted) in sample #2

$\left| \dfrac{x_1}{n_1} - \dfrac{x_2}{n_2} \right| = $ absolute proportion difference (no minus sign in difference)

$n_1 = $ size of sample #1

$n_2 = $ size of sample #2

If the sample/sample ratio is greater than 2, then we can say with 95 percent confidence that the two samples' proportions are significantly different.

For our example:

x_1 = number of up readings in sample #1 = 245
x_2 = number of up readings in sample #2 = 314
n_1 = size of sample #1 = 550
n_2 = size of sample #2 = 650

Sample/sample test ratio

$$= \frac{\left| \dfrac{245}{550} - \dfrac{314}{650} \right|}{\sqrt{\left(\dfrac{245 + 314}{550 + 650} \right)\left(1 - \dfrac{245 + 314}{550 + 650} \right)\left(\dfrac{1}{550} + \dfrac{1}{650} \right)}} = 1.302$$

Since 1.302 is less than 2, we can *not* conclude, with 95 percent confidence, that the two samples are different. Note that this is not saying that the two samples are the same! We just don't have data sufficient to say that they are different. This is similar to a jury finding a defendant not guilty because the evidence was not sufficient to reach a guilty verdict. It does not mean that the defendant is necessarily innocent.

Summary

Proportional data require much larger sample sizes than variables data to see statistically significant change. So, for example, when collecting data on a stock price change, if you have a choice of documenting the *degree* of price change or whether it went up or down, always choose to document the degree of change.

- Proportional data are based an attributes, like good-bad, up-down, and greater-lesser.
- You can compare two proportional samples or a sample with a population.

Part 3

Quantitative Evaluation of Stocks, the Market, and Investing Practices

I n Part 3, now that we know how to use various quantitative methods, we start applying them in analyzing stocks, the stock market, the economy, and consumer practices.

Chapter 8: Is a Stock or the Stock Market Overpriced?

- Price/dividend ratio
- Irving Fisher formula

Chapter 9: Using Investment Analysis to Estimate When an Economic Bubble Will Break

- Recognizing a bubble by using government data
- Recognizing a bubble by using company data
- You are unlikely to sell a stock at its high

Chapter 10: The U.S. Consumer Has Been Reducing Savings, Drawing Out Home Equity, and Increasing Debt. So, Should an Investor Be in the Stock Market?

- Getting more spending money by reducing the spending rate
- Getting more spending money by drawing out home equity
- Getting more spending money by building up debt
- So, what about being in the stock market
- Index funds versus mutual funds
- Dollar averaging

Chapter

8

Is a Stock or the Stock Market Overpriced?

No matter what the price of the stock market, there are always money managers, brokers, and many others saying that the stock market is not overpriced. They often support this view by showing that the price/earnings ratio of some index like the S&P 500 is in line with historical levels. As I am writing this book in 2007, this same argument is being used.

This and later chapters challenge the assumption that the stock market is always a great buy or that any specific stock is a great investment opportunity. If it seems that this book is always assuming that the glass is half empty, your observation is correct. With the thousands of investment options available, you should consider only stocks or other investments that best survive a critical analysis. This is especially important, given that stock promoters and companies are always pushing the positive aspects of stocks in general or a company's own stock.

How Do You Determine Whether the Stock Market is Overpriced?

To determine if the stock market is overpriced, let's look at Figure 8.1, a graph of the S&P 500 price/earnings ratio since 1960 and see if my argument that the market is overpriced is supported by data.

Price/ Earnings Ratio
The stock price divided by its annual, after-tax, per-share earnings

From Figure 8.1, a case can certainly be made that the price/earnings ratio is back to what it was in the 1960s and substantially lower than it was in the late 1990s just before the drop in stock prices in 2000.

Now, in Figure 8.2, let's look at a graph of the S&P 500 price/dividend ratio since 1960.

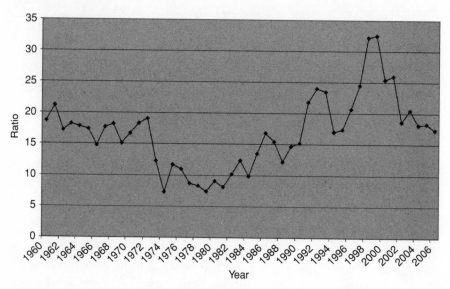

FIGURE 8.1 S&P 500 Price/Earnings Ratio

Source: Data from Bloomberg (http://pages.stern.nyu.edu/...) and S&P

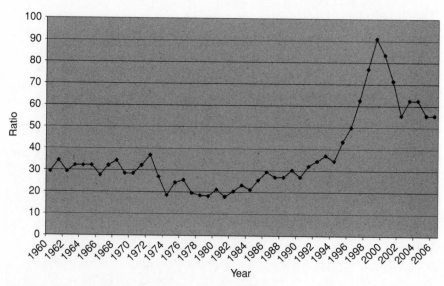

FIGURE 8.2 S&P 500 Price/Dividend Ratio

Source: Data from Bloomberg (http://pages.stern.nyu.edu/...) and S&P

Figure 8.2 tells us a completely different story than Figure 8.1 tells. In fact, in Figure 8.2 it appears that the price/dividend ratio is more than twice as high as it was in the 1960s and 1970s. It isn't as outrageous as it was in the late 1990s, but it is still historically very high. The data in Figure 8.2 are yearly, but if we looked at daily data we would see that the price/dividend ratio regularly dropped below 15. I couldn't show individual days on the plot because the more than 16,000 individual points would be too crowded.

> **Price/ Dividend Ratio**
> The stock price divided by the annual dividend paid on that share of stock

Now, some people say that the dividend philosophy of companies changed in the mid-1990s. They will tell you that companies no longer prioritize dividends; they keep the profits and reinvest them to build more value in the company, making the stock price rise. Let's see if this is substantiated by the numbers. If that reasoning is correct, we should see a substantial reduction in actual dollar dividends starting in the late 1990s. Figure 8.3 shows a graph of the actual dividends.

Figure 8.3 is plotted logarithmically, so that a uniform increase in dividends would show as an upward trending straight line, which it generally does. There was a leveling off of dividends between 1998 and 2002, but if anything, there has been a slight increase in the dividend trend for the last five years.

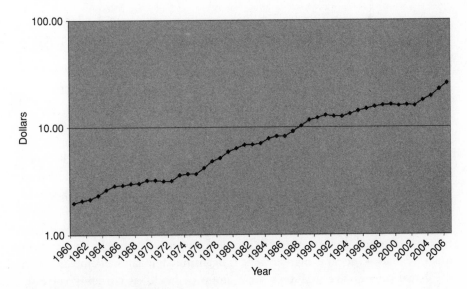

FIGURE 8.3 S&P 500 Dividends

Source: Data from Bloomberg (http://pages.stern.nyu.edu/...) and S&P

So, the argument that the price/dividend ratio is higher because of reduced dividends is not supported by the data. The only explanation is that the price of stocks is unusually high versus the dividend.

Key Point

The argument that the price/dividend ratio is higher because of reduced dividends is not supported by the data. The only explanation is that the price of stocks is unusually high versus the dividend.

The Real Way to Determine the Value of the Stock Market

As seen in these examples, it is evident that we have a conflict. Based on the price/earnings ratio, the stock market does not seem to be outrageously over-priced, yet by looking at the price/dividend ratio, the market is priced two or three times too high. We already discussed the ease of managing earnings numbers, whereas dividends are real dollars paid out to the stockholders and there-fore far more difficult to exaggerate. For those reasons, I tend to believe in the price/dividend ratio to reflect the correct price of stocks. Investment analysis is seldom definitive, but this analysis should make investors at least rethink whether they want to be in a stock market that, at least in comparison to its dividends, is historically very high priced.

Key Point

This analysis should make investors at least rethink whether they want to be in a stock market that, at least in comparison to its dividends, is historically very high priced.

Graphing is not the only way to determine the real value of the stock market or an individual stock. There is a more quantitative method. More than 70 years ago, Irving Fisher, who had been a professor at Yale, derived a way to determine the real value of a stock or a stock index, like the S&P 500. Fisher determined that a company's stock price, or a group of stocks' price, is worth its future discounted dividend stream. This is the value of its future dividends in today's dollars. Once this market value is determined, it can be compared with the actual price to see if a stock, or a group of stocks, is currently correctly priced.

> ### Key Point
>
> Irving Fisher determined that a company's stock price, or a group of stocks' price, is worth its future discounted dividend stream. This is the value of its future dividends in today's dollars.

As you may have guessed, this valuation is not without issue. Otherwise, the market prices of stocks would always be closely aligned with Fisher's valuation method, which is certainly not so.

The Irving Fisher Formula and Market Value

Irving Fisher's formula is Market Value = Current Dividend / (DR − Dividend Rate of Growth)

Irving Fisher Formula

A numerical way to determine a fair market value of a stock or the stock market in general

Let's define each term in this formula. Market value, as we discussed, is the so-called fair, or correct, price of the stock or stocks as determined by this formula. Even if someone does not accept all the assumptions inherent in this formula, the market value gives a reasonable baseline against which to evaluate a stock's price.

The current dividend is available for any stock by searching the Web. If the dividend is given as percent dividend or dividend yield, then just multiply that number times the price of the stock and divide by 100 percent. The dividend for the S&P 500 is also given on many web sites; for example, http://www.indexarb.com/dividendYieldSortedsp.html gives the dividend yield. As of November 2007, the S&P 500 dividend yield shown on this site is 1.73 percent, and the price of the S&P 500 is \$1,520. So, to get the current dividend: (\$1,520 * 1.73 percent)/100 percent = \$26.30.

The dividend rate of growth (DR) is the yield we expect from the stock market to make it an investment we would choose over a safe alternative investment, like Treasury bond yields. Between 1926 and 2000, the S&P 500 yield, including reinvested dividends, was 10.9 percent. Treasury yields in those same years averaged 5.6 percent. So the stock market earned 5.3 percent more than Treasury bonds. We will assume that this is the

Market Value

The calculated fair price of a stock or stocks, a number that provides a reasonable baseline against which to evaluate a stock's price

Current Dividend
The most recent share of profits received by a shareholder, usually stated on an annual basis

DR
The yield we expect from the stock market to make it an investment we would choose over a safer alternative investment

extra yield that investors demand from stocks to justify the added risks. Assuming that Treasury yields are currently 5 percent, this would make our DR = 5.0 percent + 5.3 percent = 10.3 percent.

We saw from Figure 8.3 that S&P 500 dividends have historically grown at a uniform rate, which happens to be 4.2 percent per year. So in the formula, the dividend rate of growth is 4.2 percent, or 0.042.

Therefore:

Current dividend = $26.30

DR = 0.103

Dividend rate of growth = 0.042

Plugging these into Irving Fisher's formula:

Market value = current dividend / (DR − dividend rate of growth)

Market value = $26.30 / (0.103 − 0.042)

Market value = $431

Now, $431 is certainly less than the current S&P 500 price of $1,520. This formula gives about the same price discrepancy we found in Figure 8.2, when we visually compared the current price/dividend ratio to the historical ratio. In fact, to match the Irving Fisher market value of $431, the stock market would have to drop 71.5 percent. This may seem impossible, but between year-end 1928 to year-end 1932, the U.S. stock market dropped 72 percent. The Japanese stock market, from 1989 through 2003, also dropped 71 percent. And remember, the 71.5 percent drop that is indicated by Irving Fisher's formula would merely take us back to a level where stock prices would be historically expected, *not* to a depression level.

The Irving Fisher Formula and GE Stock Value

Although Irving Fisher designed his formula for individual stocks, its use is valid only if you assume that a company's historical dividend growth will continue. Let's use the previous formula to check out the market value for GE. Let's first look at a graph of GE's dividends (Figure 8.4) to see if they have been growing at a constant rate. We will graph the dividends logarithmically to see if the resultant plot is an upward-trending straight line, which would indicate a value growing at a constant rate.

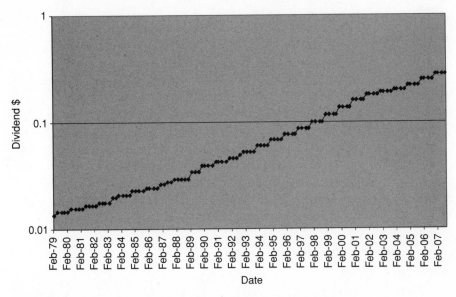

FIGURE 8.4 GE Quarterly Dividends, Plotted Logarithmically

Source: Data from http://finance.yahoo.com/

Key Point
Although Irving Fisher designed his formula for individual stocks, its use is valid only if you assume that a company's historical dividend growth will continue.

If you look closely, you will see that the dividend growth was at one rate in the 1980s, then at a higher rate in the 1990s, with a return to a somewhat slower growth rate starting in 2001. In the actual data, the rate of growth in the 1980s was 9.5 percent, 13.5 percent in the 1990s, and 10 percent since then. We will use 10 percent in our Fisher analysis. As we did for the analysis of the S&P 500, let's assume that we want a DR of 10.3 percent.

Therefore:

Current (2006) dividend = $1.03

DR = 0.103

Dividend rate of growth = 0.10

Plugging these into Irving Fisher's formula:

Market value = current dividend / (DR – dividend rate of growth)

Market value = $1.03 / (0.103 − 0.100)

Market value = $343

As stated earlier in the book, GE's current price is $41.00 per share. This formula says that *if you believe* that GE can continue its 10 percent annual growth in dividends for the long term, the per-share market value of GE stock is $343! However, as we saw in Chapter 1, recent GE sales have been going up 2.3 percent per year. As we noted earlier, GE has been great at postponing and reducing costs, but this alone will not enable them to continue with their 10 percent annual dividend growth. If their sales continue to be slow and the delayed costs start to catch up, they may have to reduce their dividend growth rate to the 4.2 percent of the general market. Let's see what GE is worth under that scenario.

Current (2006) dividend = $1.03

DR = 0.103

Dividend rate of growth = 0.042

Plugging these into Irving Fisher's formula:

Market value = current dividend / (DR − dividend rate of growth)

Market value = $1.03 / (0.103 − 0.042)

Market value = $16.89

So, if GE dividends stop growing at their unusually high rate, and they grow like the general market's rate, GE would be worth $16.89 versus its current $41.00 per share. As you just saw, Irving Fisher's formula works well for doing what-ifs, but it doesn't always give you a definitive answer!

Key Point

Some understanding of how a company is generating profits and whether dividends are likely to change is needed to make an intelligent decision on whether buying shares in a company is a good investment.

So, investors must not look at only one thing when using tools like Irving Fisher's formula. Some understanding of how a company is generating profits and whether dividends are likely to change is needed to make an intelligent decision on whether buying shares in a company is a good investment. Since dividends for the whole S&P 500 are more stable than they are for individual stocks, I value Irving Fisher's formula more for the total market than for evaluating any one stock.

Summary

It is important to determine whether a stock or the market in general is overpriced, because, like anything else you buy, at some point the price is so high that it is no longer worth buying! Although money managers, stockbrokers, and many others say that you should ignore price; you should at least be aware of an investment's price versus its historical price level before investing.

- The price/dividend ratio of a stock or the total market is valuable for historical price reference.
- The Irving Fisher formula is another way to determine the real value of an individual stock or the stock market in general.

Using Investment Analysis to Estimate When an Economic Bubble Will Break

Readers of this book are likely to have experienced the tech stock bubble of the 1990s and the housing bubble of the beginning of this century. This chapter is about recognizing a bubble, figuring out when it may break before most other investors, and profiting from this knowledge.

Bubble
When an asset's price rises so high that it becomes extremely overvalued by any reasonable economic measure

Recognizing a Bubble by Using Government Data

We already discussed the stock bubble of the late 1990s and how plotting the price of GE enabled me to judge when to sell GE stock. But the 1990s stock bubble was quickly followed by the housing bubble. When the government lowered interest rates after the terrorists' attacks on September 11, 2001 (the Fed was afraid of a recession), and mortgages became available with no documentation, nothing down, adjustable rates, and low teaser rates, a larger number of people started to compete for the available homes. To satisfy this larger market, builders

Quantitative Statistical Techniques
A method of collecting, analyzing, and interpreting data, with emphasis on numerical statistical analysis

increased the rate at which they were building new homes. Let's look at a graph, Figure 9.1, showing the new home build rate during this period.

From Figure 9.1, even though there is a natural yearly cycle embedded within the data, it appears that housing starts began to drop off in the second quarter of 2006. But let's analyze this further with some quantitative statistical techniques. This gets rather involved, so those of you less comfortable with mathematics may prefer to just use Figure 9.1 rather than doing quantitative analysis. But for those of you who want to persevere, here goes! The more information and confidence you can glean from data, the better.

First, so we can more easily do our analysis, let's take out the seasonal change. We will start with 2001 data, because it looks like that is when the volume upswing began. We will include the data through 2005, just before the upward swing leveled off. We don't want to lose all the variation within each year, just the seasonal effect. We will calculate the average for each year and then the difference of each quarter from that average. Then, we will calculate the average differences for the first through fourth quarters. We will then remove the seasonal change averages for each year based on the average differences. This is shown in Figure 9.2.

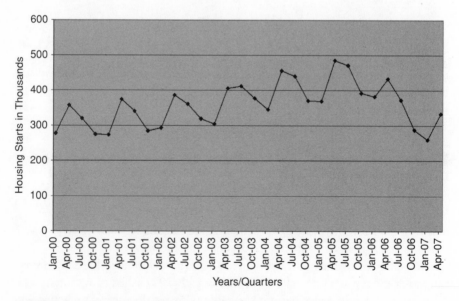

FIGURE 9.1 U.S. Housing Starts (1000s) by Quarter

Data Source: http://www.census.gov/const/quarterly_starts_completions_cust.xls

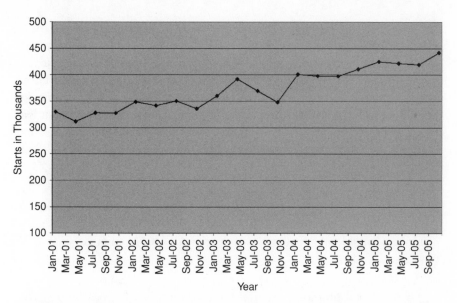

FIGURE 9.2 Quarterly Housing Starts without Seasonal Effects

Data Source: http://www.census.gov/const/quarterly_starts_completions_cust.xls

We are going to want to calculate a sigma (a measure of variation) on this data, so we want to remove the annual upward slope due to the volume increase and only look at the sigma variation over the whole period. We are removing the upward slope only for the purpose of calculating a sigma. After calculating a sigma, we will restore the upward slope for further analysis. There are other mathematical ways to do this, and if you feel comfortable with those other methods, that is fine. Our goal is to project the average housing starts for 2006 as if the upward trend had continued from the earlier years to see how the *actual* housing start data in 2006 compare with this housing starts projection.

> **Seasonal Change**
> Predictable changes that are caused by annual events and therefore not indicative of any real long-term change

When we do these calculations, it shows that, if the upward trend of housing starts would have continued, including the seasonal effects, the January 1, 2006, projected value would have been 401, and the April 1, 2006, projected value would have been 506. When we calculated the sigma (a measure of variation) for the years 2001 through 2006, without the seasonal cycle and without the volume increase, we got a sigma of 13.6.

Statistically, in a normal distribution of data, 95 percent of expected numbers would fall between the average and +/− 2 sigma. Two sigma, in this example, is

$2 \times 13.6 = 27.2$. That means that, for this study, if the *actual* housing starts for January 1, 2006, are between 401 +/−27, (between 374 and 428), then we can't be sure that the actual January 1, 2006, housing starts are significantly different than what we would have expected if the earlier upward trend had continued. And, since the actual January 1, 2006, housing starts were 382, which is between 374 and 428, we can *not* say that there is a significant change. This is consistent with our earlier observation that we couldn't see a definitive change on Figure 9.1 until April 1, 2006. Now, let's see if the April 1, 2006, numbers are significantly different than if the upward trend had continued.

Key Point

Statistically, in a normal distribution of data, 95 percent of expected numbers would fall between the average and +/− 2 sigma.

If the actual housing starts for April 1, 2006, are between 506 +/ two sigma, which is 506 +/− 27 (between 479 and 533), then we can't be sure that the April 1, 2006, actual housing starts are significantly different than what would have been expected if the earlier upward trend had continued. Since the actual April 1, 2006, housing starts were 433, which is well below the low projected value of 479, we can be sure, with 95 percent confidence, that the second quarter 2006 housing starts *are* significantly different than the projected starts if the upward trend had continued. In fact, statistically, in a normal distribution of data, 99.7 percent of expected numbers would fall between the average and +/− 3 sigma. If the actual housing starts for April 1, 2006, are outside the range of 506 +/− three sigma, which is 506 +/− 40.5 (between 465.5 and 546.5), then we can be 99.7 percent sure that the April 1, 2006, housing starts are significantly different than what we would have expected if the earlier upward trend had continued. Since the actual April 1, 2006, housing starts were 433, which is well below the low projected value of 465.5, we *can* be 99.7 percent sure that the second quarter 2006 housing starts are significantly different than the projected starts if the upward trend had continued.

Key Point

Statistically, in a normal distribution of data, 99.7 percent of expected numbers would fall between the average and +/− 3 sigma.

This could have been valuable data for any investor because of the possibility of short selling any stock that is heavily dependent on new housing. Short selling is where you sell a stock you do not own because you think the price of the stock is going to fall. To do this, by means of your broker, you borrow the stock from an existing owner, sell it, and then buy it back later so you can return the stock to its original owner. Of course, you hope to be able to buy it back at a lower price so you profit from the drop in price.

Recognizing a Bubble by Using Company Data

Companies that you could have shorted include window manufacturers, building supply stores, or the builders themselves. Although the housing starts dropped off in the second quarter of 2006, because of delays in collecting data, an investor would be unlikely to see the data until the start of the fourth quarter. The stock price of a large homebuilder, Toll Brothers, at the beginning of the fourth quarter of 2006 was approximately $30. A year later, as I am writing this book, it is $21 per share. This is a drop of 30 percent. Now, if you look at a graph of the Toll Brothers' stock price before the fourth quarter of 2006, you will see that it had started to drop even before an investor would have seen the data on housing starts. Insiders with knowledge of the builder's business would have been able to see the building starts decline before the housing data was made public, and they began selling the stock, driving down its price. Let's look at Toll Brothers' stock price, Figure 9.3, during this time interval.

> **Short Selling**
> Selling a stock you do not own because you think that the price of the stock is going to fall; to do this, by means of your broker, you borrow the stock from an existing owner, sell it, and buy it back later (you hope at a lower price), so you can return the stock to its original owner

Looking at the chart, you can see that by October 2005 there had already been a drop in price twice as large as any of the earlier price corrections. This would have enabled an investor to get a one-year jump (versus using housing start data) on short selling Toll Brothers stock or getting out of any stock related to housing! Since the stock prices are too disjointed to do an analysis similar to what we did with the housing starts data, we must look for another way to analyze this data quantitatively. The Toll Brothers graph will give us a hint. The steep drop in October 2005, when the price went down to $40, looks unique. When we look at the weekly data, which is easy to see in the historical data on http://finance.yahoo.com/, we can see that this drop was the largest weekly drop in 2005, as shown by the Figure 9.3 Toll Brothers' stock price graph.

Using the weekly price data and converting the price changes to proportions of the stock price, we get a clearer picture of the true price change effects. We can see this in Figure 9.4.

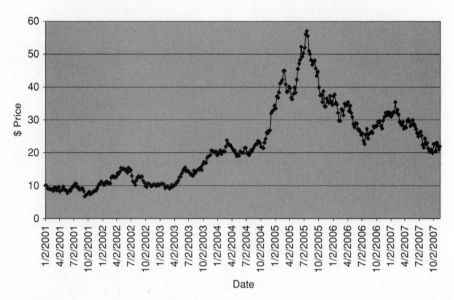

FIGURE 9.3 Toll Brothers' Weekly Stock Prices

Source: Data from http://finance.yahoo.com/

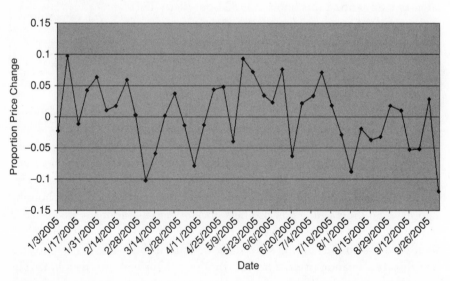

FIGURE 9.4 Weekly Proportional Change in Toll Brothers' Stock Price, 1/1/2005–10/3/2005

Source: Data from http://finance.yahoo.com/

> ## Key Point
>
> Using the weekly price data and converting the price changes to proportions of the stock price, we get a clearer picture of the true price change effects.

The proportional price change in the week of October 3, 2005, the last week in Figure 9.4, was –0.119, or –11.9 percent, which was the largest price drop in the year up to that point. The average change before October 3, 2005, in that year was 0.55 percent, and the sigma was 5.04 percent. So the average +/– 2 sigma would be 10.6 percent down to –9.5 percent. Since –11.9 percent is lower than –9.5 percent, we can be 95 percent confident that the drop of the week October 3, 2005, was larger than what would be expected from just normal variation.

Increasing Confidence with a Second Builder

One way to get a confidence level higher than 95 percent is to do the same analysis for a separate builder. If you do two independent studies, and both agree in timing and show a 95 percent probability, then the chances of the results being purely random is 5 percent × 5 percent, or 0.05 × 0.05 = 0.0025, which is very low. Let's do the analysis with another builder, Pulte Homes, whose stock price is shown in Figure 9.5.

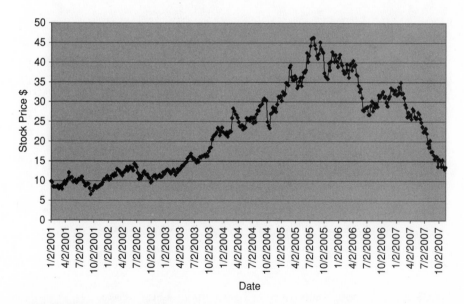

FIGURE 9.5 Weekly Stock Prices for Pulte Homes, 1/1/2001–11/15/2007
Source: Data from http://finance.yahoo.com/

Key Point

If you do two independent studies, and both agree in timing and show a 95 percent probability, then the chances of the results being purely random are very low.

Note that both Toll Brothers (Figure 9.3) and Pulte Homes (Figure 9.5) peak in the second half of 2005. So the graphs certainly correlate well. Let's look at the proportional change each week in Figure 9.6 for January 1, 2005, through October 3, 2005.

The proportional price change for Pulte stock in the week of October 3, 2005, the last week in Figure 9.5, was –0.120, or –12.0 percent, which coincidentally was about the same proportional drop that Toll Brothers' stock experienced.

Going back to the quantitative analysis of Pulte stock, the average change before October 3 in the year 2005 was 0.88 percent, and the sigma was 4.78 percent. So the average $+/-$ 2 sigma would be 10.4 percent down to –8.7 percent. Since –12.0 percent is lower than –8.7 percent, we can be 95 percent confident that the drop of the week of October 3, 2005, was larger than what would be expected from just normal variation. So given that both Pulte and Toll Brothers' stock prices dropped substantially the week of October 3, 2005,

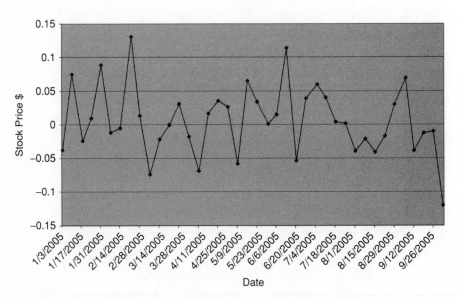

FIGURE 9.6 Proportional Weekly Change in Pulte Stock Price, 1/1/2005–10/3/2005

Source: Data from http://finance.yahoo.com/

and individually the confidences that the drops were not random were 95 percent, the fact that both happened simultaneously makes us 99.75 percent confident that these events were not random.

You Are Unlikely to Sell a Stock at Its High

Even if investors are able to recognize a bubble and sense when it is going to break, they have to accept that they are unlikely to hit the top on any stock price or the start of any substantial change in the economy unless they are lucky enough to glean conclusions about an event with specific data that is not public knowledge. Often any change is seen and acted on by insiders before any announcement is made to the public. These insiders are not necessarily managers who illegally use specific company data to buy or sell stocks. The person with inside information could be a supplier who receives an order cancellation or a UPS delivery person who notices a drop in shipments. There are always people privy to information that is not accessible to people not involved in the industry. That is why, like in the example on the housing bubble, tracking stock prices and/or volumes of a company affected by an event usually gives you an earlier warning than waiting for specific data to be released by the government or any other source.

Key Point

Even if investors are able to recognize a bubble and sense when it is going to break, they have to accept that they are unlikely to hit the top on any stock price or the absolute start of any substantial change in the economy unless they are lucky enough to glean conclusions about an event with specific data that is not public knowledge.

I mentioned before that an investor can gain from early information of an event by buying stocks in a company likely to gain from a positive event or by short selling the stock of a company likely to lose from a negative event. For those investors who feel that short selling stocks is risky, as a minimum this kind of analysis would have probably kept investors from buying stock in any industry related to new housing in that time period, because they had data to indicate that the housing bubble was breaking. Sometimes, knowing industries to stay away from is almost as valuable as knowing what areas may be attractive investments.

Key Point

Sometimes, knowing industries to stay away from is almost as valuable as knowing what areas may be attractive investments.

Note that, in 2007, many government officials, including former Fed chief Greenspan, were saying that they could not see the housing crash coming. Yet, using the very simple investment analysis tools just shown, it was obvious in 2005 that the housing bubble was breaking! And by evaluating even more builders and housing suppliers, the confidence of this finding could have been raised to an extremely high level.

Summary

Bubbles are much more obvious than people want to acknowledge. Many government officials and investors want to pretend that the world has changed and outrageous prices will go on forever. But the methods shown in this chapter enable you to unemotionally recognize bubbles and their eventual breaking. A wise investor can profit from this knowledge.

- Recent government data, when compared with historical data, can often highlight the existence of a bubble and give signs of its breaking.
- Analyzing the stock prices of companies directly involved with products affected by the bubble will often give an investor an earlier warning than the government data.

10

Chapter

The U.S. Consumer Has Been Reducing Savings, Drawing Out Home Equity, and Increasing Debt. So, Should an Investor Be in the Stock Market?

People have been spending more than they earn! This chapter gives a very brief overview on how reduced savings, excessive debt, and the breaking of the housing bubble will force people to reduce spending. Therefore, given that the stock market is at a relatively high price, is it wise to be in the market? If the consumer is forced to reduce spending, the whole market is likely to be negatively affected. **Consumer spending is responsible for approximately 70 percent of the GDP (gross domestic product)**, so any reduction can greatly slow the economy. And when the economy slows, most companies' stocks drop in price, no matter how good a company is.

> **Gross Domestic Product**
> The total value of all the goods and services produced in a country in a given year

111

Index Funds
Enable
investors to
buy stocks in
the same bal-
ance as the
stocks in a
particular
index, with no
attempt to
evaluate the
individual mer-
its of each stock
within the index

**Dollar
Averaging**
Buying a
specific dollar
amount of
stock each
month mathe-
matically
makes the
average price of
the stock pur-
chased lower
than the overall
average price of
the stock,
because fewer
shares are
bought when
the stock price
is high and
more shares are
bought when
the stock price
is low

For those investors who decide to stay in the market or plan to come back in once the market drops, this
chapter discusses the advantages of index funds versus
actively managed mutual funds. Dollar averaging is also
explained, with its upside while saving and its potential
downside when funds are being withdrawn at a uniform
dollar rate during retirement.

Getting More Spending Money by Reducing the Savings Rate

One of the ways consumers began spending extra money
was by reducing their rate of saving. The savings rate in
the United States (Figure 10.1) went down 12 of the 14
years from 1992 through 2006. Using the BINOMDIST
in Excel, you can see that the chance of this being random is only 0.0065, or about 0.65 percent. So it looks as
though people were deliberately reducing their savings to
get more cash.

Since the savings rate is now effectively zero, consumers can no longer use a reduction in savings rate to
get additional spending money. Unless they can find
another source of extra funds, consumers will have to
slow their spending.

Getting More Spending Money by Drawing Out Home Equity

Besides reducing savings, another way people were getting extra funds was by withdrawing some of their
increasing home equity. However, if we look at how
much homes were increasing in value the six years
between 2000 and 2006 versus their historical increases,
by 2006 home prices were 26 percent higher priced than
would be expected if homes had appreciated at their
historical rate. At some point, homes would just be too
expensive to buy, so it was obvious that this could not go
on forever. All of this was obvious *before* the housing
bubble broke in 2005 and 2006. All anyone had to do
was look at the data!

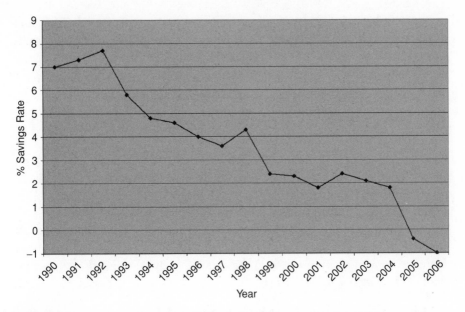

FIGURE 10.1 U.S. Savings Rate (Percent of Disposable Income), 1990–2006

Source: EBRI Databook on Employee Benefits, http://www.ebri.org/pdf/publications/books/databook/DB.Chapter%2009.pdf

Why did house prices go up so excessively in the first place? Well, just as what happened to stocks in the 1990s, the increased demand drove up prices. But with interest rates now higher, foreclosures going up, and mortgages harder to get, the demand is down, and so are home prices. Since home owners can no longer draw out home equity, they will have to slow their spending.

Home Equity

The value of a home minus the amount owed on a home

Getting Extra Spending Money by Building Up Debt

By every measure, the consumer has been building up debt. The financial obligations ratio, which is the ratio of monthly payments versus after-tax income, is now at the highest level since the Federal Reserve Board started publishing this data almost 30 years ago. And the household debt, as a percent of disposable income, is at 135 percent, which is also a high. At some point the consumer cannot afford any more debt.

Financial Obligations Ratio

The ratio of monthly payments versus after-tax income

With the savings rate at zero, excess home equity no longer available, and overall debt nearing a maximum, consumers will have to slow down their spending. This will then slow the economy, and the stock market is likely to respond with a large drop!

So, What About Being in the Stock Market?

The current mantra of those promoting stocks is to buy and hold, with no regard for stock prices, and many people follow this advice! Stocks may be the only item that so many people buy with no regard for cost. Yet, with some preliminary analysis, it can be shown that staying out of the stock market when its price is historically very high is more profitable than being in the market at all times. This statement is not universally accepted, but it is what my data show. Here are some of the findings from the detailed analysis included in my earlier book *The Second Great Depression*.

Key Point
Stocks may be the only item that many people buy with no regard for cost. Yet, with some preliminary analysis, it can be shown that staying out of the stock market when its price is historically very high is more profitable than being in the market at all times.

An assumption made in the study is that an inflation-adjusted amount of money is invested each year. The trigger that tells an investor when to buy or sell stocks is the price/dividend ratio of the S&P 500. The price/dividend ratio of the S&P 500 is the inverse of the dividend yield, which can be found at http://www.indexarb.com/dividendYieldSortedsp.html. Stock purchases are assumed to be in an S&P 500 index fund. When investment funds are not in stocks, they are assumed to be in TIPS (Treasury inflation protected securities). TIPS have been available only since 1997, but for the study it is assumed that they were an investment option *before* 1997. TIPS can be purchased directly from the government (www.publicdebt.treas.gov) for no fee. They can also be purchased like a stock through ETFs (exchange traded funds). TIPS pay a set interest rate (studied at both 1.5 percent and 3 percent). In addition to paying interest, the base purchase value of TIPS is adjusted semiannually, based on the inflation rate.

Data from 1911 through 2003 were analyzed. Here is the formula that was used for the study: Buy stocks whenever the S&P 500 price/dividend ratio is at or below 17.2. Not only will new investment money be used to buy stocks, but any accumulated TIPS will be sold and the funds used to buy stocks. When the price/dividend ratio goes above 17.2, stop buying stocks and start buying TIPS. If the price/dividend ratio goes above 28, sell all stocks that have been accumulated, and use the funds to buy TIPS.

Using this investment formula, when the investment window is assumed to be *five* years long, we find that using the formula, versus just staying invested in the S&P 500 stocks for the whole period, 72 percent of the time the formula equaled or beat the exclusive S&P 500 stock investment. The average gain by using the formula versus investing in the S&P 500 exclusively was 1.9 percent per year. Also, by using the formula, 47 percent of the time the investor was completely out of the market, therefore reducing risk.

When the investment window is assumed to be *10* years long, we find that by using the formula, versus just staying invested in the S&P 500 stocks for the whole period, 66 percent of the time the formula equaled or beat the exclusive S&P 500 stock investment. The average gain by using the formula was 0.9 percent per year versus investing in the S&P 500 exclusively. Also by using the formula, 48 percent of the time the investor was completely out of the market, therefore reducing risk.

Finally, when the investment window is assumed to be *20* years long, we find that by using the formula versus just staying invested in the S&P 500 stocks for the whole period, 66 percent of the time the formula equaled or beat the exclusive S&P 500 stock investment. The average gain by using the formula was 0.6 percent per year versus investing in the S&P 500 exclusively. Also by using the formula, 47 percent of the time the investor was completely out of the market, thereby further reducing risk.

As you can see, the per-year advantage of using the formula diminishes as the number of investment years increases. This is consistent with the generally accepted wisdom that market risk diminishes as the number of years of being invested increases. However, the real world is that few investors keep their money invested as long as they plan. Emergencies, education costs, and just plain living costs often cause investors to have to withdraw past savings sooner than their planned investment window. The fact that the formula worked so well at shorter investment windows takes away some of the risks of having to withdraw funds early.

Key Point

The per-year advantage of using the formula diminishes as the number of investment years increases. This is consistent with the generally accepted wisdom that market risk diminishes as the number of years of being invested increases.

Market Timing
Attempting to buy at a stock's low price and sell at its high

These data certainly indicate that the idea that someone should buy stock regardless of its price doesn't stand up to investment analysis. Not only does the risk go up with high-priced stocks, so does the likelihood that investors will get higher profits by putting their money in a nearly risk-free investment like TIPS.

Note that the formula discussed is *not* the same as what people commonly refer to as market timing. When people try to time the market, they are often attempting to buy at a stock's low price and sell at its high, and they are therefore in and out of a stock frequently. Studies have shown that people who try this often end up doing the opposite: selling low and buying high. No one knows how to time the market, and that includes professional traders. The difference in this approach is that it is built on the assumption that anything, including stocks, can be priced so ridiculously high as to be just too expensive, and one of the ways to measure relative price is to compare it with historical price/dividend data. After all, at some stock price, investments other than stocks become better choices. So the formula just helps investors be out of the market when it is relatively high priced and in the market when it is historically in its normal price/dividend range.

Stock Index
A measure of the performance of a select group of companies

Index Funds versus Actively Managed Mutual Funds

A stock index is a measure of the performance of a select group of companies. The composition of this select group of companies is often designed to be representative of the market as a whole. For example, the change in value of the 30 stocks in the Dow Jones Industrial Stock index, whose companies are picked by journalists at the *Wall Street Journal*, is often given on financial news broadcasts as being indicative of the total stock market. A stock index *fund* enables investors to buy stocks in the same balance as the stocks in a particular index. For example, buying shares in an index fund based on the Dow Jones is buying shares in all the companies in the Dow Jones index and in the same proportion. An index fund makes no attempt to evaluate the individual merits of each stock within the index, so the management costs of running an index fund are quite low compared with those of an actively managed mutual fund, where the charges are generally between 1 percent and 2 percent.

Stock Index Fund
Enables investors to buy stocks in the same balance as the stocks in a particular index

On the average, actively managed mutual funds perform *worse* than the market as a whole and worse than index funds. I won't supply the supporting analysis here because it is covered in countless books, such as Gregory Baer and Gary Gensler's *The Great Mutual Fund Trap* and William Bernstein's *The Four Pillars of Investing*.

Key Point

On the average, actively managed mutual funds perform worse than the market as a whole and worse than index funds.

There are more than 1,000 actively managed mutual funds in the United States. Note that this number does not include those that were shut down because their performance was so pitiful! Let's give the remaining mutual funds the benefit of the doubt that they have a 50-50 chance of beating the market in any one year. So, with this probability, what are the chances, on a purely random basis, that one of the 1,000 mutual funds will beat the market 10 years in a row? Well, let's use Microsoft Excel's BINOMDIST to find out. In BINOMDIST, Number_s = 10, Trials = 10, Probability_s = 0.5, and Cumulative = False. The rounded-off answer is 0.001. Now, since there are more than 1,000 mutual funds, each with a 1/1,000 chance of beating the market 10 years in a row, it is likely, by random chance alone, that one of them will indeed beat the market 10 years in a row. That remarkable mutual fund will get much attention and analysis by so-called experts trying to understand the investment philosophy that gave such remarkable results. And of course, investors will flock to buy stock in this great mutual fund. Data show that this fund will have less than a 50 percent chance of beating the market the following year, because it will have the burden of so much new investment money that it cannot buy stocks without driving up the price of the stock it is buying!

Key Point

Data show that this (remarkable) fund will have less than a 50 percent chance of beating the market the following year, because it will have the burden of so much new investment money that it cannot buy stocks without driving up the price of the stock it is buying.

Dollar Averaging

Dollar averaging is an effective way of accumulating stocks by buying a fixed dollar amount of stocks on a regular basis, often either monthly or with each paycheck. People with 401(k) savings plans are getting the benefits of dollar averaging without being aware of it. This is a manner of market timing in that you are buying more shares of a stock when the price is low and fewer shares when the price is high. The net effect is that, over a period of time, you will have bought stock at less than the mathematical average price of that stock over that same period of time. Here is how this works. Let's assume that over a year you buy $100 worth of a company's stock every month. During that time period, assume that the stock price has averaged $10, with some variation around that average. Here in Table 10.1 are the monthly prices of that stock, the number of shares purchased, the average price of the stock over the one-year period ($10.00), and the average purchase price per share ($9.83).

Now, this almost seems magical. But it works because, rather than buying a *constant number of shares* each month, which would have caused the average purchase price over the year to be $10.00, a *constant dollar amount of stock* was purchased each month.

Just so no one thinks that this is a free lunch, this same phenomenon often bites people when they retire and want to withdraw a constant amount of money from their stock savings each month. For example, assume an investor has their retirement savings in stocks, and the stock average price is $10.00 per share over a year, just as in the previous example. This retiree withdraws $100 per month for the whole year. Let's see what the average share price is for each share of stock sold. (See Table 10.2.)

TABLE 10.1 Saving Example Stock Price, Number of Shares, Average Purchase Price

Month	$ Stock Price	# Shares Purchased	Average Stock Price	Average Purchase Price
1	9	11.11	$10.00	$1200/122.07 = $9.83
2	11	9.09		
3	10	10.00		
4	12	8.33		
5	10	10.00		
6	8	12.50		
7	9	11.11		
8	10	10.00		
9	12	8.33		
10	8	12.50		
11	10	10.00		
12	11	9.09		
		Total = 122.07		

TABLE 10.2 Withdrawing Example Stock Price, Number of Shares, Average Sell Price

Month	$ Stock Price	# Shares Sold	$ Withdrawn	Average Stock Price
1	9	11.11	100.00	$10.00
2	11	9.09	100.00	
3	10	10.00	100.00	
4	12	8.33	100.00	**Average Selling Price**
5	10	10.00	100.00	$1200/122.07 =
				$9.83
6	8	12.50	100.00	
7	9	11.11	100.00	
8	10	10.00	100.00	
9	12	8.33	100.00	
10	8	12.50	100.00	
11	10	10.00	100.00	
12	11	9.09	100.00	
		Total = 122.07	Total = $1200.00	

The retiree sold each share for an average of $9.83, which, not surprisingly, is the same amount the saver in the earlier example paid using dollar averaging. So, dollar averaging works in reverse when someone wants to pull a constant amount from a stock fund on a regular basis, in that stocks are sold for less than the market average. Many retirees get in trouble with this. And of course, this gets even worse if the retiree is in a falling stock market or if the retiree's investments are not earning what was expected. The withdrawal of a constant amount of money exacerbates any problem with the stock price because of the need to sell additional shares when the stock price is low.

Summary

By every measure, U.S. consumers are overextended with debt and will have to slow their spending. This will slow the economy and cause unemployment to rise. The stock market, which is now historically high priced, will then drop. So, being in the stock market right now may not be the best choice.

However, for those who do plan to stay in the market, index funds have performance advantages over the average actively managed mutual fund. Also, those people who use dollar averaging as a means of saving should be aware that, if at some point they decide to withdraw a uniform amount of money each month (like during retirement), the advantage of dollar averaging is turned on its head, and the price of stocks sold becomes less than the average stock price.

- The savings rate is zero, home equity is no longer available, and consumer debt is maxed out. This will cause the consumer to slow spending.

- The lower spending rate will increase unemployment and hurt company profits.

- The stock market, which is priced higher than it has been historically, is likely to drop dramatically. It may not be the best place to be until the market drops substantially.

- Index funds have historically outperformed actively managed mutual funds.

- Dollar averaging, in which a uniform amount of money is regularly saved, causes the average price of a purchased stock to be lower than the market average. This reverses when a uniform amount of money is taken out on a regular basis.

Part 4

Specific Analysis Issues Related to Retirement Investing

S aving for retirement is extremely difficult, not only in its doing but also in quantifying the amounts required. The chapters in Part 4 enable you to work through the details and come up with specific numbers.

Details on how these retirement numbers were derived are in the Appendix.

Chapter 11: Quick-Use Baseline Retirement Numbers

- Overview discussion of retirement needs
- Baseline retirement savings
- Annual savings requirements for future retirees
- Adjustments to baseline savings requirements
- Assumed after-tax retirement budgets

Chapter 12: Adjustments for a Pension, a Lower Savings Level, or a Reduced Retirement Budget

- Option 1: Don't retire before age 70
- Option 2: Assume that you won't live beyond age 91
- Option 3: Live with, or be supported by, your children
- Option 4: Plan on a reduced retirement budget

- Pension adjustment
- Lower retirement budget adjustment

Chapter 13: Assumptions/Rationale in Savings Calculations

- Why stock market yields of 10 percent aren't assumed
- Savings to be included
- Why primary home value is not included as retirement savings
- Social Security in the future
- Roth IRAs
- Pensions and annuities
- Retirement income needs
- Company IRAs

11

Quick-Use Baseline Retirement Numbers

We have all seen the TV images: the good-looking older couple, he suave in tux, she thin in evening gown, walking barefoot along the beach. They are congratulating themselves on how, with the help of their stockbroker, they have made all the right investments over the years. They have reached financial independence and will live happily ever after with health and wealth. Retiring in Florida, they will take regular vacations to Europe, cruise to Alaska, and belong to an exclusive golf club. And of course, their beautiful children and grandchildren will just adore them, and all of this because of their financial acumen.

This is just advertising fiction. Few of us will look that good at retirement time, and the beach is likely be strewn with trash and the sky overcast! More important, few of us have made the right investment decisions over the years; in fact, most of us have not been disciplined at all in our savings and are ill-prepared for retirement. In the United States, the average savings rate has gone from 8 percent of income in 1990 to a zero savings rate in 2006. And this dearth of savings is occurring just prior to the surge of baby boomer retirements. The average boomer has only $50,000 saved for retirement. In fact, when boomers are polled, many just say that they probably will never be able to retire. The comfortable retirement images so often portrayed in financial institution advertisements just don't reflect reality.

> ### Key Point
>
> The average boomer has only $50,000 saved for retirement. In fact, when boomers are polled, many just say that they probably will never be able to retire.

However, this chapter shows that, through a combination of a delayed retirement and a realistic look at retirement needs, most people can pull off a happy and fulfilling retirement. But it will require some realism in expectations and savings needs.

An Overview Discussion of Retirement Needs

Getting Started in Investment Analysis doesn't attempt to address how much savings it would require to live the luxurious retirement lifestyle fantasized in advertisements. But this book *does* give those who are interested in planning for retirement some idea of how much they should be saving, or should have already saved, to be able to have a comfortable retirement. It also shows that, for those who are approaching retirement with too little savings, the emphasis has to be on retiring later and limiting retirement expenses, because these two things are generally in the retiree's control.

At first glance, the required retirement savings shown in this book may be overwhelming. Retirement is not inexpensive! And the accumulated savings needed to support a retirement of 30 or so years is substantial. Since many people don't even *think* about saving for retirement until at least age 35, for every year they have left to work they must be preparing for one year of retirement. The retirement savings burden is even greater for those who delay saving until after age 35 or who want to retire early.

Most people are aware of the importance of starting to save for retirement early in their careers, but that awareness doesn't help them in determining *how much* they should be saving each year or *how much* they will need at the time of retirement. Those are difficult numbers to ascertain. One recent article said simply that you need a million dollars to retire. That kind of flippant advice does little to help someone determine meaningful retirement savings.

The idea that people should be able to retire when they still have many productive years ahead of them is a relatively new concept. Certainly it wasn't a given before 1945. Life expectancy and the age at retirement were such that most people did not live all that long after they retired. And the years they had left weren't expected to be filled with days of golf and travel. Instead, they were often spent living with and being supported by their children.

But attitudes about retirement have changed. Most everyone now feels that society entitlements and personal funding should be sufficient for them to retire while they still have the health and desire to pursue a satisfying life that doesn't involve work subjugation and without having to be supported by their children. The personal funding requirement to fulfill this goal is the subject of Part 4 of this book.

Since no one can exactly predict the future, no book, computer program, or money manager can give someone a guaranteed exact retirement savings amount. Not only are future required expenses not precisely known but what a reasonable retirement goal is varies dramatically between individuals. Also, unless someone is extremely wealthy, no one can prepare for possible catastrophic health care costs. That said, people still need some general idea of what their retirement savings should be; otherwise, how do they have any chance of planning for retirement? The goal of this book is to give retirement savings estimates such that a person, or couple, could live at a comfortable level to age 100 (or an optional age 91) with a high probability of not running out of retirement funds.

After looking at this book's general guidelines, many people will realize they need to adjust their retirement savings, their planned date of retirement, or their desired retirement budget. Since no one can predict how long they will live, ideally we must look at the possibility of living to age 100. Even though the probability of living to age 100 is low, for a couple who are 60 years old, there is a 2 percent chance that one of them will live to the age of 100. In the past, people have often not planned for an extended life. Because of that, a disproportionate number of current retirees (10 percent) are living below the poverty line. One of the goals of this book is to help people analyze their retirement planning so they don't join that impoverished group.

Determining retirement savings is not easy because it requires dealing with the future value of money and other calculations that make most people's minds hurt. It requires making some allowance for inflation and some estimate of what investments will earn in the future. Some retirement incomes go up with inflation, like Social Security, and some benefits are fixed, like most company pensions. People must also make some prediction about the future of Social Security retirement benefits. The general savings guidelines in this book do this for you. The details of the assumptions that were used to generate this book's guidelines are discussed in Chapter 13.

This chapter gives general savings requirements for a comfortable retirement without unnecessary detail. But many people will look at the numbers in this chapter and

Social Security
A U.S. federal program that includes retirement benefits

Pension
A sum of money regularly paid as a retirement benefit

conclude that they just can't get there. So, the next chapter gives suggestions on how people can retire with less than this chapter's recommended target savings, gives specific adjustments for those with pensions, and provides adjustments for people wishing to modify the book's assumed retirement budgets.

Some readers won't accept the retirement savings guidelines in this book. They will find some financial planner who will promise them fantasy returns on their investments that supposedly will enable them to live their desired retirement lifestyle with fewer savings. Of course, the only desired lifestyle likely to be satisfied in the long run is the financial planner's! Brokers and money managers often assume high stock market yields, they underestimate the disastrous effects of inflation on fixed-income sources like company pensions, and they make no allowance for any future changes in our underfunded Social Security retirement program. People want to believe that they can retire with little savings, so money managers have a ready group of gullible potential customers. And it will take many years for the naive retiree to see if the promised high yields really happen. In the meantime, the money manager still receives the fees with or without the promised high investment yields.

Key Point

Brokers and money managers often assume high stock market yields, they underestimate the disastrous effects of inflation on fixed-income sources like company pensions, and they make no allowance for any future changes in our underfunded Social Security retirement program.

Retirees are often not realistic about how retirement expenditures must be budgeted, especially with regard to inflation. The initial retirement savings amount is likely to be the highest savings they have accumulated in their lives, and it can give them a false sense of security. Some people travel and spend profusely early in their retirement before they become aware of how fast they are draining their funds. They are then forced to dramatically reduce their living standards to survive the remaining years. Sadly, recovering from excessive spending in the first few years of retirement is often impossible.

Retirees often convince themselves that the companies they work for will miss them so much that they will call them back as consultants, enabling the retiree to maintain a part-time earnings source. Seldom does this happen. Also, some retirees plan on getting part-time work at a low-pressure job in a different field. Some surveys show that as many as 75 percent of retirees expect to work after retirement. The problem is that the jobs available for retirees often generate little pride or earnings. And with the influx of baby boomers, many of whom have similar work plans, these jobs will be in short supply. Wal-Mart can use just so many greeters! Generally, people are far better off extending their work years with their current employers rather than counting on part-time work after they retire.

In this book, retirement expenditure numbers are assumed to be adjusted up each year with inflation. In this way, the retiree's relative lifestyle remains constant. The base assumption is that once savings run out, home equity can be tapped to maintain a given lifestyle for another seven years or so. People who don't own their homes will not have home equity to fall back on when their other savings are gone, so they will either have to save more or just accept that they will not have the excess equity funds available.

To use this book, you must identify which of three earnings groups pertains to you.

1. High-wage earners (above $90,000 working income per year before taxes) account for 15 percent of wage earners.

2. Above-average wage earners ($50,000 to $90,000 working income per year before taxes) are 25 percent of workers.

3. Average wage earners (below $50,000 working income per year before taxes) are the remaining 60 percent.

These three earnings groups have different retirement needs, out of both choice and circumstance.

High-wage earners often have some defined costs, such as real estate taxes and utility costs, which are far higher than those in the lower-earning groups. These higher costs necessitate higher retirement budgets. Theoretically, the higher wage earners could downsize at retirement and adjust to the lower budget of an average wage earner, but their prior lifestyles make it highly unlikely that they would choose to do that unless absolutely required. Also, the Social Security benefits of each of the three earnings groups vary dramatically. The much lower Social Security benefits of those in the average earnings group means that they must save relatively more than those in the higher earnings groups to have a comfortable level of retirement income.

A few general notes on using this book: Ages, incomes, pensions, and other factors will probably not exactly match any of the reference groupings shown. Just use the grouping or numbers that are closest, or estimate between two spanning numbers. Any resultant error will be small in comparison with the many future unforeseeable financial events. Each chart is followed by one or more examples that illustrate the use of the data.

Current retirement savings should include the after-tax value of a 401(k) retirement plan, stocks, bank accounts, *excessive* equity value in a primary or secondary home (more than needed for a downsized and acceptable home), equity in rental property, and the like. Do *not* include savings slated for other things. If savings are likely to be used to pay for a child's college education or a new car, they should not be included in retirement savings.

This book assumes that the Social Security full retirement age will be raised to age 70 by the year 2016. This will make Social Security self-sustainable. Details are in Chapter 13.

Baseline Retirement Savings

Some people may find the savings requirements in this chapter frightening and unobtainable, even though the savings support a rather lean retirement budget. But don't panic! In Chapter 12 there is advice for those who just can't get to the savings levels shown in this chapter. So readers should not accept that retirement is not possible; hang in there.

The baseline savings and retirement numbers in this chapter have no provision for company pensions. Since twice as many people now rely on personal savings plans than on traditional pensions, the retirement savings numbers in this chapter will apply to most people. Table 11.1 gives the *total required savings* for most people who are planning to retire soon without a pension. Tables 11.2 through 11.7 give the *annual required savings* for those who will be retiring *in the future* without a pension. This chapter assumes that a person wants to be able to live to 100 without running out of funds. A reduced assumed lifespan is

TABLE 11.1 Total Retirement Savings for People Retiring Soon without a Pension

Required After-Tax Savings

Age at Retirement: Before-Tax Working Incomes	Age 60	Age 65	Age 70
Couples:			
High Income (over $90,000)	$560,000	$385,000	$220,000
Above-Average Income ($50,000 to $90,000)	$445,000	$310,000	$165,000
Average Income (below $50,000)	$350,000	$250,000	$145,000
Single Individuals:			
High Income (over $90,000)	$510,000	$395,000	$250,000
Above-Average Income ($50,000 to $90,000)	$365,000	$270,000	$166,000
Average Income (below $50,000)	$440,000	$350,000	$260,000

Go down the "Age at Retirement" column (Age 60, 65, or 70) and find the appropriate "Working Income" row on the left (High, Above-Average, or Average) within the appropriate Couples or Individuals group. The values within the table are the required after-tax savings at the time of retirement. Note that the amount of any mortgage must be added to the after-tax retirement savings requirements shown in the table.

shown as an option in Chapter 12, along with pension and other adjustments to these baseline savings. This chapter also shows the retirement budgets assumed in this book.

The differences in the after-tax savings amounts between the different groups in Table 11.1 don't always look logical because they are influenced by age at retirement, Social Security benefits, and retirement budgets.

> **Example 1:** The 65-year-old Johnson couple has no pension and no debt and wants to retire soon. Their combined working income is $70,000 per year, before taxes. Using Table 11.1, they see that they should have $310,000 in after-tax savings to have a reasonably comfortable retirement.
>
> **Example 2:** Mary is single and 70 years old. She has no pension, earns $45,000 per year, has a $100,000 mortgage on her home, and wants to retire soon. Using Table 11.1, Mary needs to have $260,000 + $100,000 (for the mortgage) = $360,000 in after-tax savings to have a reasonably comfortable retirement.

Annual Savings Requirements for Future Retirees

Tables 11.2 through 11.7 show annual savings requirements (to be indexed up each year with inflation) for people with no current retirement savings and no future pension. Savings requirements are divided into those for couples and those for single individuals.

Couples

The following three sections discuss the annual savings requirements for couples who want to retire in the future.

Couples Who Want to Retire at Age 60 This section and its related table show the annual savings requirements for a couple who wants to retire in the future at age 60. We assume that there are no prior savings. To use the table, couples first estimate their current combined total before-tax income. They then pick their average age, to the nearest fifth year. Then, from the numbers within Table 11.2, they can determine their annual after-tax savings requirements.

> **Example:** The Jones couple plans to retire when they reach age 60. They make $105,000 per year before taxes, which puts them in the high wage category. They are 35 years old with no retirement savings and no company pension. Table 11.2 shows that they should be saving $19,777 per year after taxes. This will index up every year with inflation.

TABLE 11.2 Couples Retiring in the Future at Age 60 with No Pension and No Current Retirement Savings: Annual After-Tax Savings Requirements

Current Age	Years until Age 60	Before-Tax Working Income		
		High Wage (over $90,000)	Above-Average Wage ($50,000–$90,000)	Average Wage (under $50,000)
55	5	$134,868	$106,879	$82,563
50	10	$ 62,374	$ 49,629	$38,338
45	15	$ 38,706	$ 30,674	$23,696
40	20	$ 26,623	$ 21,293	$16,449
35	25	$ 19,777	$ 15,763	$12,177

Go down the "Before-Tax Working Income" column (High, Above-Average, or Average) and find the closest "Current Age" line. The numbers within the table are the annual after-tax savings requirements.

Couples Who Want to Retire at Age 65   This section and its related table show the annual savings requirements for a couple who wants to retire in the future at age 65. We assume that there are no prior savings. To use the table, couples first estimate their current combined total before-tax income. They must then pick their average age, to the nearest fifth year. Then, from the numbers within the Table 11.3, they can determine their annual after-tax savings requirements.

TABLE 11.3 Couples Retiring in the Future at Age 65 with No Pension and No Current Retirement Savings: Annual After-Tax Savings Requirements

Current Age	Years until Age 65	Before-Tax Working Income		
		High Wage (over $90,000)	Above-Average Wage ($50,000–$90,000)	Average Wage (under $50,000)
60	5	$92,208	$73,766	$58,437
55	10	$47,533	$38,026	$29,808
50	15	$29,379	$23,503	$18,423
45	20	$20,394	$16,315	$12,789
40	25	$15,097	$12,078	$ 9,467
35	30	$ 9,686	$ 7,749	$ 6,074

Go down the "Before-Tax Working Income" column (High, Above-Average, or Average) and find the closest "Current Age" line. The numbers within the table are the annual after-tax savings requirements.

Example: The Smith couple plans to retire when they reach age 65. They make $75,000 per year before taxes, which puts them in the above-average wage category. They are 40 years old with no retirement savings and no company pension. Table 11.3 shows that they should be saving $12,078 per year after taxes, an amount that will index up every year with inflation.

Couples Who Want to Retire at Age 70   This section and Table 11.4 show the annual savings requirements for a couple who wants to retire in the future at age 70. It is assumed that there are no prior savings. To use the table, couples first estimate their current combined total before-tax income. They must then pick their average age, to the nearest fifth year. Then, from the numbers within Table 11.4, they can determine their annual after-tax savings requirements.

Example: The Harvey couple plans to retire when they reach age 70. They make $45,000 per year before taxes, which puts them in the average wage category. They are 45 years old with no retirement savings and no company pension. Table 11.4 shows that they should be saving $6,061 per year after taxes. This will index up every year with inflation.

TABLE 11.4   Couples Retiring in the Future at Age 70 with No Pension and No Current Retirement Savings: Annual After-Tax Savings Requirements

| Current Age | Years until Age 70 | Before-Tax Working Income | | |
		High Wage (over $90,000)	Above-Average Wage ($50,000–$90,000)	Average Wage (under $50,000)
65	5	$50,561	$40,449	$33,924
60	10	$29,243	$23,395	$19,084
55	15	$18,075	$14,460	$11,795
50	20	$12,547	$10,037	$ 8,188
45	25	$ 9,288	$ 7,430	$ 6,061
40	30	$ 5,959	$ 4,767	$ 3,889
35	35	$ 4,872	$ 3,898	$ 3,180

Go down the "Before-Tax Working Income" column (High, Above-Average, or Average) and find the closest "Current Age" line. The numbers within the table are the annual after-tax savings requirements.

Key Point

Note the huge effect of a delayed retirement. For example, a 35-year-old average-wage couple planning to retire at age 60 needs to be saving $12,177 per year. Retiring at age 65 requires saving $6,074 per year. Delaying retirement until age 70 reduces annual savings to $3,180 per year!

Single Individuals

The following three sections discuss the annual savings requirements for single individuals who want to retire in the future.

Single Individuals Who Want to Retire at Age 60 This section and its related table show the annual savings requirements for single individuals who want to retire in the future at age 60. It is assumed that there are no prior savings. To use the table, individuals first estimate their current before-tax income. Then, on the left side of the table, they must then find their age, to the nearest fifth year. Finally, from the numbers within Table 11.5, they can determine their annual after-tax savings requirements.

> **Example:** Mary, who is single, plans to retire when she reaches age 60. She makes $80,000 per year before taxes, which puts her in the above-average wage category. She is 35 years old with no retirement savings and no company pension. Table 11.5 shows that she should be saving $12,531 per year after taxes, which will index up every year with inflation.

TABLE 11.5 Individuals Retiring in the Future at Age 60 with No Pension and No Current Retirement Savings: Annual After-Tax Savings Required

Current Age	Years until Age 60	Before-Tax Working Income		
		High Wage (over $90,000)	*Above-Average Wage ($50,000–$90,000)*	*Average Wage (under $50,000)*
55	5	$116,495	$84,967	$96,187
50	10	$ 54,094	$39,454	$44,664
45	15	$ 33,434	$24,386	$27,606
40	20	$ 23,209	$16,928	$19,163
35	25	$ 17,181	$12,531	$14,186

Single Individuals Who Want to Retire at Age 65   This section and its related table show the annual savings requirements for single individuals who want to retire in the future at age 65. It is assumed that there are no prior savings. To use the table, individuals first estimate their current before-tax income. Then, on the left side of the table, they must then find their age, to the nearest fifth year. Finally, from the numbers within Table 11.6, they can determine their annual after-tax savings requirements.

> **Example:** Sam, who is single, plans to retire when he reaches age 65. He makes $40,000 per year before taxes, which puts him in the average wage category. He is 40 years old with no retirement savings and no company pension. Table 11.6 shows that he should be saving $11,785 per year after taxes, which will index up every year with inflation.

Single Individuals Who Want to Retire at Age 70   This section and its related table show the annual savings requirements for single individuals who want to retire in the future at age 70. It is assumed that there are no prior savings. To use the table, individuals first estimate their current before-tax income. Then, on the left side of the table, they must then find their age, to the nearest fifth year. Finally, from the numbers within Table 11.7, they can determine their annual after-tax savings requirements.

TABLE 11.6   Individuals Retiring in the Future at Age 65 with No Pension and No Current Retirement Savings: Annual After-Tax Savings Required

Current Age	Years until Age 65	Before-Tax Working Income		
		High Wage (over $90,000)	*Above-Average Wage ($50,000–$90,000)*	*Average Wage (under $50,000)*
60	5	$86,214	$61,549	$76,071
55	10	$43,178	$31,095	$37,105
50	15	$26,687	$19,219	$22,934
45	20	$18,525	$13,341	$15,920
40	25	$13,714	$ 9,876	$11,785
35	30	$ 8,798	$ 6,336	$ 7,561

Go down the "Before-Tax Working Income" column (High, Above-Average, or Average) and find the closest "Current Age" line. The numbers within the table are the annual after-tax savings requirements.

TABLE 11.7 Individuals Retiring in the Future at Age 70 with No Pension and No Current Retirement Savings: Annual After-Tax Savings Required

Current Age	Years until Age 70	High Wage (over $90,000)	Above-Average Wage ($50,000–$90,000)	Average Wage (under $50,000)
65	5	$55,349	$37,787	$55,171
60	10	$29,545	$20,621	$27,796
55	15	$18,261	$12,745	$17,180
50	20	$12,676	$ 8,847	$11,926
45	25	$ 9,384	$ 6,550	$ 8,828
40	30	$ 6,020	$ 4,202	$ 5,664
35	35	$ 4,923	$ 3,436	$ 4,631

Go down the "Before-Tax Working Income" column (High, Above-Average, or Average) and find the closest "Current Age" line. The numbers within the table are the annual after-tax savings requirements.

Example: George, who is single, plans to retire when he reaches age 70. He makes $100,000 per year before taxes, which puts him in the high wage category. He is 50 years old with no retirement savings and no company pension. Table 11.7 shows that he should be saving $12,676 per year after taxes, which will index up every year with inflation.

Key Point

Again, note the huge effect of a delayed retirement. For example, a 40-year-old above-average-wage individual planning to retire at age 60 needs to be saving $16,928 per year. Retiring at age 65 will require saving $9,876 per year. Delaying retirement until age 70 reduces annual savings to $4,202 per year!

Adjustments to the Annual Baseline Savings Requirements

The prior annual savings tables assumed no preexisting savings. Table 11.8 enables people with after-tax savings to reduce their annual savings requirements by the amount shown. This table applies to both couples and individuals. Simply subtract the amount shown within the table from the baseline annual savings amounts identified in Tables 11.2 through 11.7.

TABLE 11.8 Annual Savings Reduction per $10,000 in Existing After-Tax Savings	
Years until Retirement	*Annual Savings Reduction per $10,000 in Existing After-Tax Savings*
5	$2,250
10	$1,200
15	$ 850
20	$ 700
25	$ 600
30	$ 450
35	$ 400

Example: Mike, who is single, plans to retire when he reaches age 70. He makes $100,000 per year before taxes, which puts him in the high wage category. He is 50 years old with $50,000 in after-tax retirement savings and no company pension. Table 11.7 showed that, without retirement savings, he should be saving $12,676 per year after-taxes. However, Table 11.8 shows that he can reduce his annual savings by $700 for every $10,000 he has in after-tax retirement savings. Since his savings are $50,000, he can reduce his annual savings by 5 × $700 = $3,500. This makes his required annual savings $12,676 − $3,500 = $9,176. This amount will index up every year with inflation.

Assumed After-Tax Retirement Budgets

As you have seen in these examples, the breakdown of expenses within each after-tax retirement budget varied widely among the people I polled, and the proportions often changed as the retiree aged. However, the totals shown are representative of the group average. See Table 11.9.

TABLE 11.9 Retirement Budgets			
	Before-Tax Working Income		
	High Wage (over $90,000)	*Above-Average Wage ($50-000–$90,000)*	*Average Wage (under $50,000)*
COUPLES			
Food	$9,000	$8,000	$7,000
Restaurants/entertainment	$3,000	$2,000	$1,000
Utilities	$4,000	$3,000	$3,000

(continued on next page)

TABLE 11.9 (Continued)

	Before-Tax Working Income		
	High Wage *(over $90,000)*	*Above-Average Wage* *($50-000–$90,000)*	*Average Wage* *(under $50,000)*
COUPLES			
Miscellaneous household	$ 5,000	$ 4,000	$ 2,000
Automobile	$ 8,000	$ 6,000	$ 4,000
Medical	$ 7,000	$ 6,000	$ 5,000
Vacations/travel	$ 4,000	$ 3,000	$ 2,000
Real estate taxes/insurance	$ 5,000	$ 4,000	$ 3,000
Clothes and miscellaneous	$ 5,000	$ 4,000	$ 3,000
Couples' After-Tax Budgets	**$50,000**	**$40,000**	**$30,000**
INDIVIDUALS			
Food	$ 7,000	$ 6,000	$ 6,000
Restaurants/entertainment	$ 3,000	$ 2,000	$ 2,000
Utilities	$ 4,000	$ 3,000	$ 3,000
Miscellaneous household	$ 4,000	$ 3,000	$ 3,000
Automobile	$ 6,000	$ 5,000	$ 5,000
Medical	$ 4,000	$ 3,000	$ 3,000
Vacations/travel	$ 4,000	$ 2,000	$ 2,000
Real estate taxes/insurance	$ 4,000	$ 3,000	$ 3,000
Clothes and miscellaneous	$ 4,000	$ 3,000	$ 3,000
Individuals' After-Tax Budgets	**$40,000**	**$30,000**	**$30,000**

Go down the appropriate "Working Income" column (High, Above-Average, Average) and read the value opposite either **"Couples' After-Tax Budgets"** or **"Individuals' After-Tax Budgets."** These values are the annual after-tax retirement budgets.

Example: The Kline couple is ready to retire. Their earnings are $60,000 per year. From Table 11.9, they see that they will need a $40,000 annual after-tax retirement income for a reasonably comfortable retirement,

As I mentioned at the beginning of this chapter, if you find that you just can't get the savings shown in this chapter, don't give up. Chapter 12 gives savings and budget options for those without pensions, as well as adjustments for those expecting a pension or wishing to make other adjustments to their retirement plans.

Summary

Required baseline savings are shown for people retiring soon, and annual savings are shown for those retiring in the future. These baseline savings assume that there is no pension, which is true for two-thirds of retirees. An adjustment to the baseline savings is given for people with existing savings. The assumed retirement budgets are shown.

Although these savings requirements should be the minimum goal, for many people these savings amounts just won't be possible for various reasons. In the next chapter is a discussion on various options for these people.

- Savings are shown for three different income groups and for three different retirement ages.
- The retirement budgets are also shown for three different income levels.
- The next chapter gives options for those people who can't save the suggested baseline amounts.

12

Adjustments for a Pension, a Lower Savings Level, or a Reduced Retirement Budget

Even though the savings and retirement budgets shown in Chapter 11 are lean and everyone should strive to that level of savings as a minimum, some readers may find that, for various reasons, the savings numbers in Chapter 11 are just unattainable or not appropriate. So, we have to figure the best way to use whatever retirement savings are available.

In this chapter, we look at delaying retirement to age 70. We examine the effect on required savings if it is assumed that the retiree will live no longer than age 91. Living with your children is an option, the retiree may be able to live on a reduced budget, or you may have a pension that reduces your savings needs.

Option 1: Don't Retire before Age 70!

For many people, retirement before the age of 70 is just not going to be feasible. For people who are having trouble saving for retirement, this should be the first adjustment to the retirement plan.

Let's look again at the total retirement savings requirements for the three earnings groups, assuming age 70 retirement, in Table 12.1.

TABLE 12.1   Total Retirement Baseline Savings Requirements (from Chapter 11) for the Three Earnings Groups, Assuming Age 70 Retirement

Age at Retirement: 70	
Before-Tax Working Incomes	Required After-Tax Savings
Couples:	
High income (over $90,000)	$220,000
Above-average income ($50,000 to $90,000)	$165,000
Average income (below $50,000)	$145,000
Single Individuals:	
High income (over $90,000)	$250,000
Above-average income ($50,000 to $90,000)	$166,000
Average income (below $50,000)	$260,000

Key Point

For many people, retirement before the age of 70 is just not going to be feasible. For people who are having trouble saving for retirement, this should be the first adjustment to the retirement plan.

Because, as mentioned earlier, the average baby boomer has $50,000 saved, even at a retirement age of 70, these numbers look out of reach for many wannabe retirees. Let's look at several additional options.

Option 2: Assume That You Will Not Live Longer Than Age 91

The baseline savings in Chapter 11 were calculated by assuming that the retiree would live to age 100, with savings not running out until age 93, and home equity then carrying the retiree to the age of 100. Option 2 assumes that someone is willing to risk running out of savings *before* age 93. Based on data from the Social Security Period Life Tables, a person aged 70 has an 11 percent chance of living to age 91 or older. An individual who is willing to take an 11 percent chance of outliving savings and home equity can plan for running out of savings at age 84, with home equity then carrying the retiree until age 91. After age 91, the retiree would only have Social Security as income, which is extremely tight living. For a couple, this means that there would be a 20 percent chance that one of them would live beyond the target age of 91. This lower length of life assumption reduces the Chapter 11 calculated savings. Table 12.2 shows how this acceptance of a lower life expectancy affects required savings.

An 11 percent chance that an individual could run out of savings and a 20 percent chance that a couple could run out of savings are not trivial. And the reduced savings requirements still exceed the average $50,000 retirement savings of baby boomers. Because of that, it is time to talk about the 10,000-pound elephant in the room, which is the option of living with or being supported by your children if you run out of retirement funds.

Key Point

An 11 percent chance that an individual could run out of savings and a 20 percent chance that a couple could run out of savings are not trivial.

Option 3: Live with, or Be Supported by, Your Children

Almost 10 million baby boomers are currently raising their children or support-ing an adult child while assisting an aging parent financially, according to the Pew Research Center. And that trend is likely to grow as baby boomers retire with insufficient funds. Living with your children in the autumn years of your

TABLE 12.2   Total Savings Assuming a Retiree Will Run Out of Funds and Home Equity at Age 91 or at Age 100

	Funds and Home Equity Run Out at	
Couple	Age 91	Age 100
High wage required savings	$150,000	$220,000
Above-average wage required savings	$115,000	$165,000
Average wage required savings	$100,000	$145,000
Individual		
High wage required savings	$170,000	$250,000
Above-average wage required savings	$115,000	$166,000
Average wage required savings	$180,000	$260,000

This table assumes age 70 retirement and the same retirement budgets shown in Chapter 11. The numbers within the table are the required after-tax retirement savings.

life was the way it was done in the past and is likely to become quite common-place in the future. Retirees' budget needs go down substantially if they live with their children in retirement. Their housing and utility costs are basically eliminated, and additional food costs are much lower than what was assumed in our retirement budgets. In fact, the addition of a retiree's income, even if it is only Social Security, often assists the household in which the retiree lives! So, if both you and your children are emotionally amenable to having you live with them in your later years, a very real option is to not worry too much about run-ning out of funds. Your children become a very real backup plan, and if you are really lucky, this option comes with a lot of love thrown in as a bonus!

Key Point

Retirees' budget needs go down substantially if they live with their children in retirement.

However, let's proceed as if living with, or being supported by, one's chil-dren is not a desirable option. As was seen earlier, the savings requirements in Table 12.2, even with the lowered life expectancy of age 91, exceed the $50,000 retirement savings of the average baby boomer.

Option 4: Plan on a Reduced Retirement Budget

Another option available for those who have not saved sufficiently is to lower their retirement budget such that the reduced savings are sufficient. Table 12.3 shows two retirement budgets that make this happen for someone retiring at age 70 with no pension and an assumption of a reduced life expectancy of age 91. The two reduced savings levels shown are $100,000 and $50,000. I also show the assumed value for Social Security alone, which would be the retirement budget for someone with zero retirement savings.

Key Point

Another option available for those who have not saved sufficiently is to lower their retirement budget such that the reduced savings are sufficient.

Some of these budgets seem ridiculously low. However, at the time I am writing this, the minimum wage is $5.15 per hour. Someone working full time at that hourly rate would make $10,700 per year, and that is before taxes. Even

TABLE 12.3   Retirement Budgets for Retirement Savings of $100,000, $50,000, and No Savings (the Same as Assumed Social Security Retirement Benefits)

	$100,000 Savings	$50,000 Savings	Zero Savings
Couple			
High wage retirement budget	$45,000	$41,000	$37,000
Above-average wage retirement budget	$38,000	$34,000	$30,000
Average wage retirement budget	$30,000	$25,000	$21,000
Individual			
High wage retirement budget	$33,000	$29,000	$25,000
Above-average wage retirement budget	$28,000	$24,000	$20,000
Average wage retirement budget	$23,000	$18,000	$14,000

The table assumes age 70 retirement and a life expectancy of age 91. The numbers within the table are the reduced after-tax retirement budgets, which will index up each year with inflation.

with the proposed increase of the minimum wage to $7.25 per hour over the next two years, the annual income would only be $15,080. From this table, we can see that an average-wage individual, retiring with $50,000 savings, will have an annual income of $18,000 after taxes and that income will go up every year with inflation. That retirement income is greater than the working income of many people. I don't mean to say that this is a generous amount of money, but it is more than people earn who are working at minimum wage.

Example 1: A-65-year-old high-wage couple (working wages over $90,000 per year) wants to retire soon. From Chapter 11, they determine that they must have $385,000 in savings to retire comfortably at age 65. Since they only have $50,000 saved, they see that they will have to delay retirement to age 70 and assume a life expectancy of age 91. Assume that by the time they reach 70, they have $100,000 saved, which is below the $220,000 that is specified in Chapter 11 and in Table 12.1. So the couple realizes that they will not be able to have the $50,000 retirement budget that is available for those who retire at age 70 with the $220,000 recommended savings. Using Table 12.3, they see that with their $100,000 savings they are able to have an after-tax retirement budget of $45,000 per year. This is tighter than the $50,000 baseline retirement budget, but it is very livable.

Example 2: A 70-year-old man is ready to retire. He is in the average wage group (less than $50,000 before-tax income). He sees from Chapter 11 that he should have $260,000 saved. He only has $50,000 saved, but he is willing to live on a much reduced retirement budget and assume a life expectancy of age 91. From Table 12.3, he can see that his retirement budget is only $18,000 per year, versus the $30,000 recommended for a comfortable retirement. Although this is a low budget, it is $4,000 higher than just Social Security retirement benefits alone. And since people *do* live on Social Security alone, the extra $4,000 per year makes retirement somewhat more feasible.

Given the smaller retirement budgets shown here, it is important to discuss what is important about retirement. I am going to be presumptuous enough to say that it is *freedom* and *well-being*. The retiree wants the freedom to not have to report to work every day. He or she may be tired of taking directions from what appears to be a teenage boss. The 70-year-old retiree is also likely to be starting to feel the bones creak, and an afternoon nap is often just the right cure. The well-being part of retirement doesn't just refer to health. Well-being also includes not having to worry on a daily basis about how payments are going to be met and having enough money for food and medicine.

Key Point

The well-being part of retirement doesn't just refer to health. Well-being also includes not having to worry on a daily basis about how payments are going to be met and having enough money for food and medicine.

Most people, by the time they reach age 70, have realized that a new car and fancy house just aren't all that important, and they will sacrifice those if that is the difference of being able to retire with some degree of dignity and affordability. Also, they have learned that chicken or a pork loin that is seasoned properly can taste every bit as good as steak, and the differences between a low-cost wine and an expensive one are often lost by the second sip. Indeed, I know several retired people who have a lot of savings but choose to live on little more than their Social Security every month. And these people seem no less happy than those living a far more luxurious retirement lifestyle.

Adjusting for a Pension and Different Retirement Budgets

Before referencing this section, go back to Chapter 11 and determine your baseline savings (without any adjustments for pensions or modified retirement budgets). The baseline savings from Chapter 11 are what we are adjusting here.

Pension Adjustments

All of the earlier savings tables assumed that there was no company pension, which is true for most people. However, for those few still fortunate enough to have a pension, this section shows how much the prior baseline savings can be reduced.

Table 12.4 shows how much the Table 11.1 baseline savings for couples or individuals retiring soon can be reduced if they have a pension. This table is applicable for those with both fixed and inflation-adjusted pensions and for people retiring at age 60, 65, or 70. Examples following the table clarify it.

Couples or Individuals Retiring Soon with a Pension Scheduled to Start at Age 65

> **Example 1:** Mary and John are a 60-year-old couple. They have a $20,000 per year after-tax fixed pension that is planned to start at age 65. Per Table 12.4, the pension will enable them to reduce their savings by 8 × $20,000 = $160,000. They earn $110,000 per year, have no mortgage on their home, and want to retire soon. From Table 11.1, they need $560,000 (baseline savings) − $160,000 (pension reduction) = $400,000 in after-tax savings to have a reasonably comfortable retirement with a $50,000 per year after-tax retirement budget.

TABLE 12.4   Pension Adjustments for Couples or Individuals Retiring Soon with a Pension Scheduled to Start at Age 65

Couples or Individuals Retiring Soon at Age 60

Fixed annual pension	Subtract 8 times the after-tax amount of a *fixed* annual pension from the amount of baseline savings from Table 11.1
Inflation-adjusted annual pension	Subtract 16 times the after-tax amount of an *inflation-adjusted* annual pension from the amount of baseline savings from Table 11.1

Couples or Individuals Retiring Soon at Age 65 or 70

Fixed annual pension	Subtract 13 times the after-tax amount of a *fixed* annual pension from the amount of baseline savings from Table 11.1
Inflation-adjusted annual pension	Subtract 20 times the after-tax amount of an *inflation-adjusted* annual pension from the amount of baseline savings from Table 11.1

Example 2: Grace is single and 70 years old. She has a $10,000 per year after-tax fixed pension that was originally planned to start at age 65. Per Table 12.4, the pension will enable her to reduce her savings by 13 × $10,000 = $130,000. She earns $45,000 per year, has a $100,000 mortgage on her home, and wants to retire soon. From Table 11.1, Grace needs $260,000 (baseline savings) + $100,000 (for the mortgage) − $130,000 (pension reduction) = $230,000 in after-tax savings to have a reasonably comfortable retirement with a $30,000 per year after-tax retirement budget.

Couples or Individuals Retiring in the Future with a Pension Scheduled to Start at Age 65 Table 12.5 displays the annual savings reduction per $10,000 of an after-tax fixed pension that is scheduled to begin at age 65. Subtract the amount in Table 12.5 from the baseline after-tax amount of annual savings that was determined for those without pensions (Tables 11.2 though 11.7). People with inflation-adjusted pensions can subtract twice the amount shown in Table 12.5.

Example: Hank, who is single, plans to retire when he reaches age 70. He makes $100,000 per year before taxes, which puts him in the high wage category. He is 45 years old with no retirement savings. He has a $10,000 after-tax fixed pension scheduled for age 65, but Hank won't start the pension until he retires at age 70. Table 11.7 showed that his baseline annual retirement savings are $9,384 per year after taxes. However, per Table 12.5, his expected pension allows him to reduce these savings by $1,600 per year. So, his adjusted annual after-tax savings will be $9,384 − $1,600 = $7,784. This will index up every year with inflation.

TABLE 12.5 Annual Savings Reduction per $10,000 of After-Tax Fixed Pension

Current Age	Planned Retirement Age		
	60	65	70
65			$21,800
60		$20,950	$ 8,500
55	$13,600	$ 8,200	$ 4,430
50	$ 5,300	$ 4,300	$ 2,600
45	$ 2,800	$ 2,500	$ 1,600
40	$ 1,600	$ 1,450	$ 870
35	$ 1,000	$ 850	$ 600

Because a fixed pension's real value goes down every year with inflation, to keep its purchasing power the same, only two-thirds of the initial pension amount should be used, with the remainder invested. Every year, the portion of the pension that is used will increase with inflation. In this way, the real effect of the fixed pension, combined with the saved portion and its earnings, will remain constant. All the calculations in this book related to fixed pensions assume that this will be done. In many cases, early in retirement, people with fixed pensions will have incomes in excess of the retirement budgets assumed in this book. However, they must be sure not to use all their available funds and to invest the excess if they wish to maintain a constant retirement lifestyle.

Key Point

Since a fixed pension's real value goes down every year with inflation, to keep its purchasing power the same, only two-thirds of the initial pension amount should be used, with the remainder being invested.

People Retiring Soon Who Require a Lower Retirement Budget

Earlier chapters gave recommended savings goals for someone retiring soon or in the future. However, some of you began your savings for retirement too late, lost money in the stock market, sent three children through Harvard, or for a myriad of other reasons did not save the money shown in the earlier chapters. As mentioned earlier in the book, people who find themselves in this situation have only two realistic options: delay retirement or be resigned to live on a lower retirement budget.

For people retiring soon, Table 12.6 shows how much you must reduce your annual retirement budget for every $10,000 less than the Table 11.1 advised total retirement savings.

TABLE 12.6 Reduction in Annual Retirement Budget for Every $10,000 in Total Savings That Are Less Than the Baseline Savings in Table 11.1

Retirement Age	Reduction in Retirement Budget
Age 60	$475 lower retirement budget for every $10,000 reduced savings
Age 65	$526 lower retirement budget for every $10,000 reduced savings
Age 70	$602 lower retirement budget for every $10,000 reduced savings

Example 1: A high-income (over $90,000 per year) couple wants to retire soon at age 65. They have no pension. From Table 11.1, they determined that the recommended total baseline retirement savings were $385,000 to have a $50,000 annual retirement income. However, the couple has only saved $305,000. They want to retire anyway, so using Table 12.6, they see that they must reduce their annual retirement budget $526 for every $10,000 in reduced savings. Since they have $80,000 less than what is recommended, they must reduce their retirement budget by 8 × $526 = $4,208. So rather than having a $50,000 annual retirement budget, their retirement budget must be $50,000 − $4,208 = $45,792. Of course, this annual amount will index up every year with inflation.

Example 2: An average-income (below $50,000 per year) individual wants to retire at age 70. This person has no pension. From Table 11.1, this individual determined that the recommended savings amount was $260,000 to have a $30,000 annual retirement income. However, this individual's total retirement savings are only $200,000. Because, from Table 12.6, the annual retirement budget must be reduced by $602 for every $10,000 in reduced savings, this individual must reduce his or her annual budget by 6 x $602 = $3,612. So rather than having a $30,000 annual retirement budget, the annual retirement budget must be $30,000 − $3,612 = $26,388. Of course, this annual amount will index up every year with inflation.

Summary

In this chapter, we looked at delaying retirement to age 70. We also saw that required savings go down substantially if it is assumed that the retiree will live no longer than age 91. Although many people don't like to consider this option, living with one's children also saves a lot of money. The retiree may be able to live on a reduced budget or have a pension that reduces savings needs.

Options for retirees with inadequate savings include the following measures.

- Delay retirement until age 70.
- Assume that you won't live beyond age 91.
- Live with your children.
- Live on a reduced budget.
- Be fortunate enough to have extra income from a pension.

13

Assumptions/Rationale in Savings Calculations

You need to know what assumptions I made in this book and the rationale for those assumptions. In this chapter, I discuss many of these. I explain that high stock market yields have not historically been the norm, so I did not assume them for the future. Primary homes have to be lived in, so their value has not been included in savings. Social Security is in trouble, so I assumed that full retirement will soon be changed to age 70. Roth IRAs are preferred for your savings vehicle because, when money is withdrawn at retirement, you won't be subject to whatever tax rate is in effect. Since most pensions are fixed, they go down in real value over time, and that effect is included in the book's tables. Retirement needs were based on interviews with acquaintances and by reading various articles. Inflation's effect on savings is an issue, but if someone is saving in a company IRA, their savings choices may not include inflation-adjusted securities.

Why Stock Market Yields of 10 Percent Aren't Assumed

Many retirement planners assume that a large portion of retirement savings will be invested in the stock market, and they assume that you will be able to get 10 percent annual yields on retirement savings. This assumption is made because that was the average yield the S&P 500 realized over the past 100 years. However, there are several problems in using this average in any calculations for *future* retirement savings yields.

First, this 10 percent average stock market yield has historically been made up of 4.5 percent dividends, 3.5 percent inflation, and a 2 percent gain in the S&P 500 market value over and above inflation. Because of the current relatively high price of stocks, dividend rates as of the beginning of 2006 for the S&P 500 were only about 1.5 percent. If the stock market value grows as it did for the prior 100 years, but with current dividend rates that are now 3 percent lower than in the past, the total yield from the stock market would be 7 percent. This 7 percent would be made up of 1.5 percent dividends, 3.5 percent inflation, and a 2 percent gain in S&P 500 value over and above inflation. Again, this is assuming that the market grows exactly as it did for the last 100 years, which is extremely optimistic given that the market is currently priced historically high. In fact, since 1997 the stock market has been generally at the highest levels it has been for 106 years, at least in relationship to its dividends. It seems that stock market has far more opportunity to go down than up.

There are many books and articles on the stock market that have come to similar conclusions. I show some of these in Table 13.1. Note that in many cases the values shown required some interpretation on my part, because the authors often gave alternative scenarios of a sudden drop in market prices, a slowly growing stock market, or no inflation.

The median (middle value) of these predictions is 7.0 percent, which is the same value we just got by looking at the effect of the current lower dividend rate.

Since most people are in the stock market through mutual funds, often in a 401(k) plan through their employer, they are paying 2 percent per year for the costs related to managing that mutual fund and the costs of buying and selling stocks within the fund. So the net gain on their stock investments will be 7 percent (the median from Table 13.1) − 2 percent (expenses) = 5 percent.

TABLE 13.1   Books and Articles Predicting Future Stock Market Yields

Books/Articles	Future Stock Yield Including 3.5 Percent Inflation
Winning with the Dow's Losers	7.0 percent
Yes, You Can Time the Market	3.5 percent
The Four Pillars of Investing	7.0 percent
Valuing Wall Street	6.0 percent
Winning the Loser's Game	7.5 percent
Financial Reckoning Day	Negative
Irrational Exuberance	4.5 percent
Robert Arnott and John Bogle Articles	7.0 to 7.5 percent

Keep in mind that the stock market yields to which we refer are averages, with huge variations over the years. For example, those who bought the S&P 500 at the end of 1999 were still well behind in their investments as of the beginning of 2006. Their investment return has been negative. And people who bought stocks in the late 1960s had to wait 20 years just to get a return that kept up with inflation. The buy-and-hold philosophy of investing in the stock market promises that if you wait long enough, you will make money in the stock market. However, if you need to withdraw money to live on, that philosophy just doesn't work. Extended periods of poor stock market performance are devastating for any retired person relying on stock market returns for income. For that reason, this book *does not* assume 10 percent stock market yields to calculate retirement savings. The stock market is too risky for someone who has no way of recovering from years of below-average market performance and whose required withdrawal of funds to live on year to year so devastates the investment value.

Key Point

If you need to withdraw money to live on, buy-and-hold just doesn't work. Extended periods of poor stock market performance are devastating for any retired person relying on stock market returns for income. For that reason, this book *does not* assume 10 percent stock market yields to calculate retirement savings. The stock market is too risky for someone who has no way of recovering from years of below-average market performance and whose required withdrawal of funds to live on year to year so devastates the investment value.

Money has never liked to work very hard. The end of the last century temporarily hid this fact, but only the very wealthy have ever been able to live solely on the earnings from their savings. You should accept the fact that consistent yields of 10 percent on your savings are probably not going to be obtainable for the foreseeable future.

This book assumes that retirement savings are in TIPS, a low-risk, conservative investment that automatically adjusts for inflation. With average inflation, it has total yields at least comparable to the projected 5 percent stock market yields. This investment choice is especially good for anyone who is concerned about high inflation or a possible stock market crash.

None of this logic precludes stocks as a possible great investment in the future. If the market took a huge dive and you were not already invested in stocks, the stock market would then again be viable. By having your savings in TIPS, which maintain the real value of your principal, you would be in a position of having capital available to take advantage of the opportunity to buy stocks at much lower prices. Given the current stock market prices and the projected yields, this book conservatively assumes that your savings are in TIPS.

Savings to Be Included When Using This Book

Current savings include the after-tax value of a 401(k) retirement plan, stocks, bank accounts, *excessive* equity value in primary home, value of second home or rental property, and similar assets. Do *not* include savings slated for other things.

Note that investments, like stocks, can suddenly change in value, as many did in 2000. And second homes may also drop in value along with the value of a primary home, as they already are with the current housing bubble bust. Because of these risks, if you want to be conservative, include only a portion of these savings' values when determining your current retirement savings.

Key Point

Note that investments like stocks can suddenly change in value. Because of these risks, if you want to be conservative, only include a portion of these savings' values when determining your current retirement savings.

Why the Value of a Primary Home Should *Not* Be Considered as Retirement Savings

In recent years, housing prices have gone up far more than inflation. However, the only way the increased value in a house can normally be realized is through selling the home, refinancing and taking out equity, or getting a home equity loan. Unless you have a huge amount of excess equity in your home, are ready to downsize in a substantial way, or intend to move from a high housing cost area to one with much lower housing prices, you usually must buy another home with a similarly inflated price. So selling a home doesn't normally free up equity. Given that interest rates are no longer at their historical lows, taking out equity through refinancing or through a home equity loan will probably increase your monthly payments. So any access to equity is largely not available, with the exceptions I listed. In general, the value of a home comes to play in the last years of a person's life, when a retiree either moves in with a relative or enters a nursing home. Then the value of the home can be used to allay expenses since no replacement home is required. But the equity is often of no help during early retirement years.

During most of your life, your primary home is an expense, not a source of financial liquidity. Wait long enough, and most homes either rot away or are demolished. This fact has been muddied in recent years when people began to think of a home as a long-term investment opportunity. The housing bubble has actually put many people's retirement goals at risk because they have begun to think of the inflated value of their homes as a store of retirement savings. When the bubble breaks, which all bubbles eventually do, people may find that their net home equity is negative.

Key Point

The housing bubble has actually put many people's retirement goals at risk because they have begun to think of the inflated value of their homes as a store of retirement savings. When the bubble breaks, which all bubbles eventually do, people may find that their net home equity is negative.

Social Security in the Future

In determining specifics on retirement savings amounts, we need to make some best guess of the future of Social Security benefits. One of the biggest advantages of Social Security retirement benefits is that they are indexed up with inflation, just like the TIPS savings I am advocating, versus company pensions and annuities, which are normally fixed at the time withdrawal is begun. Social Security retirement benefits often start out with a value less than a fixed company pension, but after years of inflation, Social Security can become the largest contributor to retirement income. Social Security is currently the major income source for many retirees. We therefore have to predict what Social Security retirement benefits will be available in the future, especially given the fact that Social Security is underfunded.

Key Point

Social Security retirement benefits often start out with a value less than a fixed company pension, but after years of inflation, Social Security can become the largest contributor to retirement income. Social Security is currently the major income source for many retirees.

Most people are aware of the coming funding crises with Social Security. The dominant issues are the forecast increase in retirees (due to aging baby boomers) and people living longer while the number of people in the worker support base will be declining. When Social Security was first implemented in 1935, the average life expectancy was less than 70. According to the Social Security Administration, life expectancy will be 80 by 2050. In 2003, there were 3.3 workers per each retiree receiving Social Security. Projections show that by 2030 there will only be two workers supporting each retiree, if the Social Security retirement plan stays the way it is. This will cause the Social Security Retirement System to run out of funds unless some changes are made in benefits, the retirement age, or the Social Security taxes of workers.

In 1983, the Social Security full retirement age was raised from 65 to 67, to be implemented slowly until 2027. This change was considered the best option after carefully considering all the alternatives. This was the first step in trying to address the issue of Social Security future funding. Delaying the retirement age not only reduces the resultant benefits (because people are on Social Security fewer years before they die) but also keeps people in the work-force longer, which addresses the problem of the proportion of workers to retirees. However, the delay in retirement age must be taken to age 70 to fully address the current funding crisis. By delaying retirement to age 70, the net effect of both the reduced number of people getting retirement benefits and the resultant larger workforce will be to increase the ratio of the number of con-tributing workers versus the number of retirees receiving Social Security in 2030 to 3.1, close to what it was in 2003!

Theoretically, there is supposed to be a fund where prior excess contribu-tions into Social Security were accumulated to pay for future retirees. But this fund has nothing but IOUs from our government, which is already dramatically in debt. Without including the IOUs, which our country has no funds to back up, the Social Security funding will go into the red sometime about 2015. You may see articles stating that Social Security is not in big trouble because it is funded through 2048 or such. These writers are assuming that the IOUs from the government are collectible. For Social Security to survive, it must be self-funding, which a delayed retirement will accomplish. In this way, the money coming in from employee and company contributions will be immediately dis-pensed to retirees before the rest of the government has a chance to spend it.

Since so many people are questioning whether Social Security will even survive, an increase in retirement age to 70 will be accepted as a necessary evil. The government has already shown its willingness to adjust the retirement age by its earlier delay of retirement to age 67. There will be years of congressional meetings and pulling of hair by Congress and the president as they examine other options, but a further delay in retirement age is what they will probably implement because that is what they did before. There will still be a reduced retirement option at age 65 but with *greatly* reduced benefits. This early-retirement option will pacify those still wanting an early out, at least until they see just how very reduced the benefits are! This book assumes that Social Security retirement benefits are not drawn until full retirement age is reached.

Given this analysis, we will assume that someone will be able to get full Social Security retirement funds (equivalent to the amount someone currently gets at age 65), but not until they are 70 years old. This book's calculations assume that this delay in retirement to age 70 is fully implemented by the year 2016.

Other Social Security retirement funding solutions all have unacceptable ramifications. For example, President Bush's proposed plan that would put some portion of current Social Security withholdings into stock market private savings plans would not only put future Social Security savings at stock market risk but also devastate the current Social Security system. The current retirement system is largely pay as you go, and current payroll withholdings are used to pay the benefits of those already retired. If you reduce the withholdings going to current retirees by removing some of the funds for stock purchases, the current system will not have enough money remaining to make payments to current retirees. Some have suggested that the government borrow the needed trillions of dollars to enable the overlap of both plans. Even Congress, which has shown little fiscal restraint in the past, is not going to fall for that! They don't want any more borrowing.

Increasing taxes on current workers to keep the current retirement age for future retirees would require doubling Social Security withholdings. This would cause a worker revolt and is politically not viable. A delay in retirement age seems like the most likely solution to the Social Security funding problems.

Roth IRAs

This book assumes that future retirement funds are saved in a Roth IRA and, as already stated, that the investment mode is TIPS. The Roth IRA is a way to control taxes on savings and their related gains. TIPS are one of the many ways that money can be invested *within* many Roth IRAs.

When funds are saved in a regular IRA (individual retirement account), the money is saved pretax, and you

IRA, Regular
Money is saved pretax, and all taxes are paid when the funds are withdrawn, generally after age 59½; taxes are then paid not only on the funds deposited but also on any gains those funds have generated

IRA, Roth
Taxes are paid up front on the funds as they are being saved, and there are no additional taxes on those funds or on any related gains when the funds are withdrawn, generally after age 59½

pay all taxes at a later date when the funds are withdrawn, generally after age 59½. Taxes are then paid not only on the initial deposited funds but also on any gains those funds may have generated. In a Roth IRA, the funds are saved *after taxes,* so taxes are paid up front on the funds as they are being saved. There are no additional taxes on those funds, *or on any of the related gains,* when the funds are withdrawn, again generally after age 59½.

The savings and withdrawal restrictions are less stringent on a Roth IRA than on a traditional IRA. But the biggest advantage for the retiree is that when savings are in a Roth IRA, you *know* how much will be available at retirement. Net savings will not be at the whim of whatever income tax rate happens to be in effect at fund withdrawal. Nor will retirees have to worry about other income that would affect their tax rate.

Key Point

The savings and withdrawal restrictions are less stringent on a Roth IRA than on a traditional IRA. But the biggest advantage for the retiree is that, when savings are in a Roth IRA, you *know* how much will be available at retirement.

Table 13.2 shows the income and contribution limits on a Roth IRA at the time I am writing. Any person or couple whose wages exceed the partial contribution wage limits in this table is not eligible for a Roth IRA.

Since all future retirement savings are assumed to be in a Roth IRA and in TIPS, concerns about taxes and inflation are reduced.

A law passed early in 2006 makes Roth IRAs even more attractive. Starting in 2010, everyone, no matter at what income level, will be able to convert a traditional IRA into a Roth IRA. You'll still have to pay the normal taxes on the traditional IRA, but at the point you convert into a Roth IRA, you will have a

TABLE 13.2   Income and Contribution Limits on Roth IRAs

	Full Contribution Wage Limit	Partial Contribution Wage Limit
Single/head of household	$ 99,000	$114,000
Married filing jointly	$156,000	$166,000
Contribution limits (per person):		
	Under age 50	Age 50 or older
2008	$4,000	$5,000
2009+	$4,000 + Inflation	$5,000 + Inflation

tax-free account. This is consistent with the tax-free assumption I used in this book to calculate the earnings on retirement savings. This conversion opportunity makes it advantageous even for those having earnings that exceed the maximum income for a deductible IRA contribution to still have a nondeductible IRA.

Pensions and Annuities

Generally, any pension payout amount is fixed at the time of retirement and stays constant throughout the retirement years. In any period with inflation, the real purchasing power of a company pension (or any fixed annuity) is essentially reduced. This is especially an issue when inflation is high. In our calculations, we assume an annual inflation rate of 3.5 percent, which will cut the real purchasing power of any pension in half in 21 years. However, in times of high inflation, for example 10 percent per year, the pension's purchasing power is reduced by 50 percent in only seven years. That is why we want all elements of our savings, other than the company pension, to be inflation-protected. That is why we specified TIPS as a savings mode. In the retirement savings calculations in this book, the diminishing effect of a pension with 3.5 percent inflation is already factored in.

    Companies generally quote any pension in the actual dollar amount the employee will receive at the time of retirement at age 65, assuming employment until then. Of course, companies estimate the pension this way because, for young employees, it makes the pension look more impressive because it takes place many years from now, hence with probable inflated dollars. The effect of inflation on diminishing the pension's purchasing power is generally not discussed by the company.

    For an example, let's look at a nominal company pension estimated by the company at $20,000 per year (after taxes) at age 65. The person with the example pension is currently 35 years old, so he or she has another 30 years to work until age 65. Let's see what that $20,000 per year is worth 30 years from now in current dollars, assuming 3.5 percent annual inflation, which is the historical average inflation. To calculate this value, divide $20,000 by 1.035, then divide that result again by 1.035. Do this 30 times, once for each year. For those familiar with Excel, this is the same as dividing $20,000 by $1.035^{30} =$ $7,125. This means that the future pension is worth $7,125 per year in current dollars. This is not a trivial amount, but the pension certainly looks less impressive than $20,000 when expressed in current dollars. Since pensions are normally estimated to begin at age 65, for those retiring at age 70 the book's retirement calculations assume an additional value over the nominal pension amount because of the five additional years of work. Similarly, for those retiring at age 60, the pension that kicks in at age 65 is slightly reduced because of the five fewer years of employment.

As we have noted, since the pension payment amount is fixed, its effective value continues to decline during retirement as inflation does its thing. All of these adjustments are already embedded in the book's calculations.

Key Point

Since the pension payment amount is fixed, its effective value continues to decline during retirement as inflation does its thing.

For those relatively few people who still have pensions, I am including a strong warning: fixed company pensions are at risk for two reasons. First, many companies are eliminating them. Even those already retired and already receiving a pension can suddenly find themselves with reduced (or no) benefits. Second, in this book's calculations, I assume 3.5 percent annual inflation. If inflation takes off as it did between 1973 and 1981, averaging 9 percent per year, the value of any fixed pension will go down 55 percent in nine years.

Key Point

Fixed company pensions are at risk for two reasons. First, many companies are eliminating them. Second, in this book's calculations, I assume 3.5 percent annual inflation. If inflation takes off as it did between 1973 and 1981, averaging 9 percent per year, the value of any fixed pension will go down 55 percent in nine years.

When I reviewed this book's content with a 65-year-old retired couple, they stated that their after-tax retirement income was approximately $48,000 per year, half from Social Security and half from a fixed company pension. They had little in savings. They observed that, although they spent all their retirement income, they felt that they were living comfortably with no financial issues. It took me some time to convince them that, given future probable inflation, they should reduce their current spending by about $8,000 per year, or a third of their pension (which would then be invested). In this way, they could index their retirement spending related to their pension every year with inflation and keep a constant lifestyle. The portion of pension that is invested will eventually be needed to supplement their actual pension amount. Otherwise, their real retirement income will go down every year because of the fixed pension that does not adjust with inflation. These retirees are currently spending more than their future real income will support.

Inflation-adjusted pensions, which are often part of government work-force benefits, don't have these negatives related to real value. However, even these pensions are at risk if government revenues go down. Even without a reduction in government revenue, many government agencies are already so overextended in future pension commitments that no one knows how these agencies will cope with the existing pension obligations.

Retirement Income Needs

When trying to determine retirement income needs, I became aware of two things. First, few retirees follow a budget. Instead, they sort of adjust their living expenses by sensing what is happening to their savings drawdown. Many retirees start retirement at a spending level that is not sustainable. Sometimes they buy new cars, take dream vacations, or dine out regularly. After all, that was their retirement dream—to live the good life! Since few retirees have bud-gets, it was difficult for me to ascertain an accurate cost of living. But I man-aged to come up with budgets by looking at their beginning-of-the-year funds, adding their income, and then subtracting their end-of-year savings. I esti-mated the breakdown of expenditures through credit card and check receipts. However, the specifics of where the money was spent were not static. Generally, as the retiree got older, less was spent on clothes, restaurant meals, and travel. Instead, more was spent on medical expenses.

The other thing I discovered when trying to determine retirement needs is that the level that people considered minimal for a comfortable retirement went up dramatically for higher-wage people, and some of this need for addi-tional funds was real because of their lifestyles. For example, the real estate taxes paid in an upscale community are substantially higher than those in lower-cost neighborhoods. Often the higher-cost neighborhoods have other community fees that are not avoidable.

Because of these differences in retirement living costs, I broke working in-come into three groups. The reason it is important to look at wage groupings is not only because of retirement income needs but also because the three earnings groups get substantially different Social Security retirement benefits. Even though the Social Security system has some degree of leveling built in, in that those who contribute less get relatively higher benefits versus their contributions, this level-ing doesn't come close to making up the difference in actual benefits. Those in higher wage brackets get much higher Social Security retirement benefits. This makes saving for a comfortable retirement much more challenging for those earn-ing low wages.

There are two groups for which this book probably has little value. Those earning minimal wages will have a very difficult time accumulating the savings recommended for the average earnings group. Many of these people already make far less than the comfortable retirement level suggested in this book. In fact, I don't fully understand how people can live on a minimum wage, much less save for retirement. The other group that probably doesn't need this book is people in the top 1 percent earnings bracket, those earning in excess of $330,000 per year. Their retirement minimums are probably above most other people's dream retirement.

Seventy to 80 percent of the prior working income is a standard estimate for retirement income needs (the estimated amount you will need per year once you retire). So, when estimating retirement needs, I tested them against that general guideline. Because of the large amount of retirement savings needed to support 70 percent of a prior working income, some of you will realize that your retirement lifestyle must be reduced to cost *far less than 70 percent of your prior income*. How much can you reduce your living costs and still live comfortably? The best way to estimate this is to start adding up all the costs of items you don't *really* need and then subtract this total from your prior working income (again, after taxes). We have become so accustomed to multiple cell phones, 100 TV channels, large high-definition televisions, several new cars, and multiple computers that it is difficult to remember that we don't really *need* these things.

If you go back and look at the retirement budget details, you will see that one of the larger expenses is automobiles. One of the biggest potential savings for retirees is to reduce to one car. Not only do you save on depreciation but also you save on insurance and, in some cases, taxes. Also, retirees who are trying to reduce their budgets should consider a car like a used Honda Civic rather than a new, more expensive automobile. Since cars are made much better than they were even a few years ago, and as a retiree you will probably be driving less, there is no reason that you cannot keep a car for 10 or more years. Saving $3,000 per year on automobiles, which is often quite doable, reduces retirement savings needs by approximately $60,000!

When you try to reduce your retirement budget, look for areas where costs can be cut with little or no resultant hardship. For example, you and your partner may like a glass or two of wine with your dinner. You normally buy $10 per bottle wine, which certainly is not extravagant. However, there are wines that experts judge as quite good that cost $5 per bottle! The resultant $1,500 saved per year reduces required savings by approximately $30,000.

Going out to restaurants is a very high cost. Couples who regularly dine out several times a week can easily save $2,500 a year by making going out to eat an exception, reducing required retirement savings by $50,000.

Food is the biggest budget item. The easiest and best savings is to eliminate junk food. Obviously this is not only good for your budget but also great for your waistline. And indeed, that will save future expenditures, especially if you exercise as well. Many health problems and related costs are greatly reduced by watching your weight and working out. Also, buying food from low-cost groceries can save 20 percent of your food budget, and in most cases you are getting exactly the same food. This can save up to $3,000 per year and reduce required retirement savings by $60,000.

Once you identify what expenses you can reduce during retirement, you then have to add in any costs that come after retirement that weren't there before, like extra health care insurance premiums that were previously paid by your employer. Health care costs in general are a big issue for the elderly. One article I read recently suggested putting away $200,000 in an account exclusively for health care costs. Perhaps, in an ideal world, this is the answer. But I sense that most readers won't be able to afford this option. Instead, I suggest that you review your own philosophies and make sure that your living will and your communications to your loved ones reflect your own philosophy on elderly health care and nursing homes. A disproportional amount of health care costs are spent on the last few years of life, and not always with joyful results. Not too many years ago, the elderly generally died at home, with loving care from their families but with no intrusive measures to extend life. Because of that, the cost of life's end in those days was far less than what it is currently, and I am not sure that the net effect wasn't kinder. What you want as far as extensive end-of-life health care will somewhat determine how much you should include in your retirement budget for potential health care costs. This choice has both philosophical and religious ramifications, so this isn't an easy decision. The $200,000 mentioned above for health care costs, however, is probably on the high side, unless someone is struck by Alzheimer's or something equivalent. Then, $200,000 may be on the low side. Again, a living will may limit even these costs.

Key Point

Once you identify what expenses you can reduce during retirement, you then have to add in any costs that come after retirement that weren't there before, like extra health care insurance premiums that were previously paid by your employer.

Company Supported Individual Retirement Accounts (IRAs)

Some companies offer IRAs. In some cases the company matches the employee's savings amount, or some portion of it. Obviously, these savings should be counted toward the savings requirements. However, if TIPS or some other inflation-adjusted investment vehicle is not an option in the plan, you will have to watch inflation levels and know that some portion of your savings is at risk because it is not indexed according to inflation.

Summary

High stock market yields have not historically been the norm, so I did not assume them for the future. Primary homes have to be lived in, so their value has not been included in savings. Social Security may be in trouble, so I assumed that full retirement will soon be changed to age 70. Roth IRAs are preferred for savings because at retirement you won't be victim to whatever tax rate is in effect. Since most pensions are fixed, they go down in real value over time, and that effect is included in the book's tables. Retirement needs were based on interviews with acquaintances and by reading various articles.

- High stock market yields are not assumed.
- The primary home value is not included as savings.
- Roth IRAs are the preferred savings vehicle.
- Fixed pensions go down in real value with inflation.
- Retirement budgets are only best estimates.

Understanding Logarithmic Charts

D ata in this book are sometimes displayed on logarithmic charts. Here is an explanation on how constant rate increases (or decreases) in data displayed in this manner will show as a sloped straight line.

For example, suppose we had something that was increasing 20 percent every year, and the initial value was 1. Table A.1 shows what the data would look like for 10 years.

Let's plot these data on regular and logarithmic graphs, Figures A.1 and A.2.

TABLE A.1 Data That Are Increasing 20 Percent per Year

Year	Value
0	1
1	1.2
2	1.44
3	1.728
4	2.0736
5	2.48832
6	2.985984
7	3.583181
8	4.299817
9	5.15978
10	6.191736

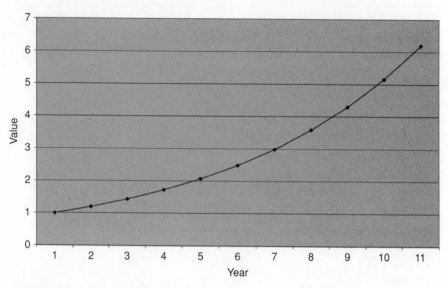

FIGURE A.1 Regular Chart, Data Growing 20 Percent per Year

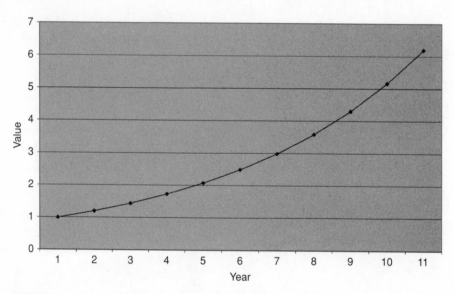

FIGURE A.2 Logarithmic Chart, Data Growing 20 Percent per Year

The reason this works is that the log is the power to which base 10 must be raised to reach a given number. For an example, see Table A.2.

10 to the zero power is 1

10 to the first power is 10

10 to the second power is 100

10 to the third power is 1,000

And so on

If you plot these numbers, you will get a curve with a dramatic upswing. However, if you plot the power, the graph will be a sloped straight line. On a logarithmic chart (actually semilog), rather than actually plotting the number, the vertical axis is spaced equivalent to the power of the number. That is why you see the unusual left-hand axis numbers on the log charts.

A logarithmic chart is useful on data that you suspect are increasing at a steady rate, like dividends increasing at a uniform rate for a number of years. The straight line on the plot tells you that this is happening.

Retirement Detail for Above-Average Wage Couples ($50,000 to $90,000 Before-Tax Income per Year)

This section is for those people who would like to see more of the detail that was used to generate the retirement charts in this book. Only the above-wage couple detail is shown, but the other retirement group tables were generated in a similar manner.

TABLE A.2   Data to the Base 10

Base	Power	Number
10	0	1
10	1	10
10	2	100
10	3	1000
10	4	10000
10	5	100000
10	6	1000000

This section applies to couples who are in the above-average wage category, which the book defines as earning $50,000 to $90,000 per year. Obviously, there is a huge earnings range within this group. However, many couples in the higher salary end of this group have not been disciplined savers, so these guidelines apply for the whole group.

Retirement Budget for Above-Average Wage Couples

Andy and Betty C. are a typical above-average wage couple who want to retire. Andy earns $70,000 per year, has made a good living throughout his career, and has been paying into Social Security every year since graduating from college. Betty has not worked many years, so she will get the spouse's Social Security benefit once she reaches eligibility age. Typical of most couples, there is no company pension, but they do have an IRA. Their home is fully paid for.

After looking at their own living expenses and talking to retired friends with similar lifestyles, they determined that they were going to require $40,000 per year, after taxes, to have a comfortable retirement. Betty had read that a person should count on needing 70 percent to 80 percent of their working income for retirement needs. They wanted to see if this budget fell into that range. Andy's $70,000 income, after discounting for 25 percent taxes, is $52,500. Their $40,000 proposed budget is 76 percent of the $52,500, which is within the target 70 percent to 80 percent of working income.

The couple wants their retirement income to index up with inflation so they can have a relatively constant lifestyle throughout their retirement. They know that inflation has historically been about 3.5 percent per year, so they plan to adjust their retirement income up each year with inflation, no matter what it is.

Andy and Betty don't want their funds to run out before the age of 93. At that point, they figure that they can borrow against their home and maintain their lifestyle for additional years until they are close to age 100. They don't see the need to plan to live longer than that, since no relative on either side of their family has lived to age 100.

Andy and Betty had been hit pretty hard in the year 2000 downturn of the stock market and don't want to count on rates of return that require high-risk investments. They are putting their savings into TIPS. Although these securities only pay about 3 percent interest, when you add in the expected 3.5 percent inflation, the total expected yield is 6.5 percent.

We will use the $40,000 first-year retirement budget in all the calculations for above-average wage couples. Of course, this budget will increase every year with inflation, which is assumed to be 3.5 percent per year in the calculations.

Sixty-Year-Old Above-Average Wage Couple Retiring Soon

A 60-year-old couple wants to retire. Since their savings are in a traditional IRA, their savings are taxable. For this example, the tax rate is assumed to be 25 percent when they transfer their savings out of their traditional IRA. Their combined Social Security benefits will be $28,800 per year (in current dollars) once they become eligible, which will adjust annually for inflation. The tax rate on Social Security is assumed to be 15 percent. As we discussed, inflation is assumed to be 3.5 percent per year, and income on their savings is assumed to be 6.5 percent per year.

Given these assumptions, how much savings do they need in their traditional IRA such that funds do not run out before age 93, which will be 33 years from now? As you will see in the Table A.3, the couple needs **$445,000 after-tax savings!** Since the couple's savings are in a traditional IRA, which is before taxes, they need $593,000 in their IRA. Table A.3 shows how the couple's savings will support their needs for 33 years, which will get them to age 93. There is no reason for you to go through this table in great detail. It is included only so you can get some idea of funds flow and some appreciation of how income and expense numbers get huge with inflation.

The years shown in Table A.3 start at the first year of retirement.

Note that their savings drop dramatically the first six years until the inflated Social Security kicks in. Retiring before being eligible for Social Security is very expensive.

If the couple had *not* had their home paid for, they would have had to add the amount they owed on their home to the required savings. For example, if this couple had a $200,000 mortgage, they would have needed $445,000 + $200,000 = $645,000 in after-tax savings to retire.

One more adjustment will be of interest for those few people who have a fixed company pension. If this couple had a company pension, the required savings could have been reduced by the amount of the annual after-tax pension multiplied by 8. So, if the couple had a $10,000 after-tax annual pension scheduled to start at age 65, the couple could have reduced their required savings by $80,000. This would have made the required savings $445,000 − $80,000 = $365,000. For someone who had a $10,000 *inflation-adjusted* after-tax pension that started at age 65, the required savings could have been reduced by the amount of the annual after-tax pension multiplied by 16. This would have made the required savings $445,000 − $160,000 = $285,000.

For couples where both spouses worked and contributed to Social Security, it is the combined income that is of interest, and the resultant combined Social Security will be close to what it is if one person is the primary wage earner and the other gets the spouse's portion. If their combined income is $50,000 to $90,000, then this section applies, and so do the calculated savings.

TABLE A.3   Savings Flow, Above-Average Wage Couple, 60 Years Old, Retiring Soon

Year	Start of Year Savings	Income on Savings	Social Security Income	Total Income	Retirement Expenses	End of Year Savings
1	$445,000	$28,925		$28,925	$40,000	$433,925
2	$433,925	$28,205		$28,205	$41,400	$420,730
3	$420,730	$27,347		$27,347	$42,849	$405,229
4	$405,229	$26,340		$26,340	$44,349	$387,220
5	$387,220	$25,169		$25,169	$45,901	$366,488
6	$366,488	$23,822		$23,822	$47,507	$342,802
7	$342,802	$22,282	$30,092	$52,374	$49,170	$346,006
8	$346,006	$22,490	$31,145	$53,636	$50,891	$348,751
9	$348,751	$22,669	$32,235	$54,904	$ 52,672	$350,983
10	$350,983	$22,814	$33,364	$56,177	$ 54,516	$352,644
11	$352,644	$22,922	$34,531	$57,453	$ 56,424	$353,673
12	$353,673	$22,989	$35,740	$58,729	$ 58,399	$354,003
13	$354,003	$23,010	$36,991	$60,001	$ 60,443	$353,561
14	$353,561	$22,981	$38,285	$61,267	$ 62,558	$352,270
15	$352,270	$22,898	$39,625	$62,523	$ 64,748	$350,045
16	$350,045	$22,753	$41,012	$63,765	$ 67,014	$346,796
17	$346,796	$22,542	$42,448	$64,989	$ 69,359	$342,426
18	$342,426	$22,258	$43,933	$66,191	$ 71,787	$336,830
19	$336,830	$21,894	$45,471	$67,365	$ 74,300	$329,896
20	$329,896	$21,443	$47,063	$68,506	$ 76,900	$321,502
21	$321,502	$20,898	$48,710	$69,607	$ 79,592	$311,518
22	$311,518	$20,249	$50,415	$70,663	$ 82,377	$299,804
23	$299,804	$19,487	$52,179	$71,666	$ 85,260	$286,209
24	$286,209	$18,604	$54,005	$72,609	$ 88,245	$270,574
25	$270,574	$17,587	$55,896	$73,483	$ 91,333	$252,724
26	$252,724	$16,427	$57,852	$74,279	$ 94,530	$232,473
27	$232,473	$15,111	$59,877	$74,987	$ 97,838	$209,622
28	$209,622	$13,625	$61,972	$75,598	$101,263	$183,957
29	$183,957	$11,957	$64,141	$76,099	$104,807	$155,249
30	$155,249	$10,091	$66,386	$76,478	$108,475	$123,251
31	$123,251	$ 8,011	$68,710	$76,721	$112,272	$ 87,701
32	$ 87,701	$ 5,701	$71,115	$76,815	$116,201	$ 48,315
33	$ 48,315	$ 3,140	$73,604	$76,744	$120,268	$ 4,791
34	$ 4,791	$ 311	$76,180	$76,491	$124,478	− $ 43,196

When a couple are two different ages, use the primary wage earner's age when looking for the applicable retirement guidelines.

Sixty-Five-Year-Old Above-Average Wage Couple Retiring Soon

A 65-year-old couple wants to retire. Since their savings are in a traditional IRA, their savings are taxable. For this example, the tax rate is assumed to be 25 percent when they transfer their funds out of their traditional IRA. Their combined Social Security benefits will be $28,800 per year, which will adjust annually for inflation. The tax rate on Social Security is assumed to be 15 percent. As we discussed, inflation is assumed to be 3.5 percent per year, and income on their savings is assumed to be 6.5 percent per year.

Given these assumptions, how much in savings do they need in their traditional IRA such that funds do not run out before age 93, which will be 28 years from now? As you will see in Table A.4, the couple needs **$310,000 after-tax savings!** Since the couple's savings are in a traditional IRA, which is before taxes, they need $413,000 in their IRA. The table shows how the couple's savings will support their needs for 28 years, which will get them to age 93. Unless you really want to, there is no reason for you to go through this table in great detail. It is included only so you can get some idea of funds flow and some appreciation of how income and expense numbers get huge when inflation is accounted for.

The years shown in Table A.4 start at the first year of retirement.

If the couple had *not* had their home paid for, they would have had to add the amount they owed on their home to the required savings. For example, if they had a $200,000 mortgage, they would have needed $310,000 + $200,000 = $510,000 in after-tax savings to retire.

One more adjustment will be of interest for those few people who have a fixed company pension. If this couple had a company pension, the required savings could have been reduced by the amount of the annual after-tax pension multiplied by 13. So, with a $10,000 after-tax annual pension, the couple could have reduced their required savings by $130,000. This would have made their required savings $310,000 − $130,000 = $180,000. With a $10,000 *inflation-adjusted* pension that started at age 65, the required savings could have been reduced by the amount of the annual after-tax pension multiplied by 20. So, if the couple had a $10,000 after-tax annual pension that rose with inflation, the couple could have reduced their required savings by $200,000. This would have made their required savings $310,000 − $200,000 = $110,000.

TABLE A.4 Savings Flow, Above-Average Wage Couple, 65 Years Old, Retiring Soon

Year	Start of Year Savings	Income on Savings	Social Security Income	Total Income	Retirement Expenses	End of Year Savings
1	$310,000	$20,150		$20,150	$ 40,000	$290,150
2	$290,150	$18,860	$25,337	$44,197	$ 41,400	$292,947
3	$292,947	$19,042	$26,224	$45,265	$ 42,849	$295,363
4	$295,363	$19,199	$27,142	$46,340	$ 44,349	$297,355
5	$297,355	$19,328	$28,092	$47,420	$ 45,901	$298,873
6	$298,873	$19,427	$29,075	$48,502	$ 47,507	$299,867
7	$299,867	$19,491	$30,092	$49,584	$ 49,170	$300,281
8	$300,281	$19,518	$31,146	$50,664	$ 50,891	$300,054
9	$300,054	$19,503	$32,236	$51,739	$ 52,672	$299,121
10	$299,121	$19,443	$33,364	$52,807	$ 54,516	$297,412
11	$297,412	$19,332	$34,532	$53,863	$ 56,424	$294,851
12	$294,851	$19,165	$35,740	$54,906	$ 58,399	$291,358
13	$291,358	$18,938	$36,991	$55,930	$ 60,443	$286,845
14	$286,845	$18,645	$38,286	$56,931	$ 62,558	$281,217
15	$281,217	$18,279	$39,626	$57,905	$ 64,748	$274,375
16	$274,375	$17,834	$41,013	$58,847	$ 67,014	$266,208
17	$266,208	$17,304	$42,448	$59,752	$ 69,359	$256,600
18	$256,600	$16,679	$43,934	$60,613	$ 71,787	$245,426
19	$245,426	$15,953	$45,472	$61,424	$ 74,300	$232,551
20	$232,551	$15,116	$47,063	$62,179	$ 76,900	$217,830
21	$217,830	$14,159	$48,710	$62,869	$ 79,592	$201,108
22	$201,108	$13,072	$50,415	$63,487	$ 82,377	$182,218
23	$182,218	$11,844	$52,180	$64,024	$ 85,260	$160,981
24	$160,981	$10,464	$54,006	$64,470	$ 88,245	$137,207
25	$137,207	$ 8,918	$55,896	$64,815	$ 91,333	$110,688
26	$110,688	$ 7,195	$57,853	$65,047	$ 94,530	$ 81,206
27	$ 81,206	$ 5,278	$59,878	$65,156	$ 97,838	$ 48,524
28	$ 48,524	$ 3,154	$61,973	$65,127	$101,263	$ 12,388
29	$ 12,388	$ 805	$64,142	$64,948	$104,807	-$ 27,471

Seventy-Year Old Above-Average Wage Couple Retiring Soon

A 70-year-old couple wants to retire. Since their savings are in a traditional IRA, they are taxable. For this example, the tax rate is assumed to be 25 percent. Their combined Social Security benefits will be $35,000 per year, which will adjust annually for inflation and is subject to an estimated 15 percent tax. The tax rate on Social Security is assumed to be 15 percent. As we discussed, inflation is assumed to be 3.5 percent per year, and income on their savings is assumed to be 6.5 percent per year.

Given these assumptions, how much savings do they need in their traditional IRA such that funds do *not* run out before age 93, which will be 23 years from now? As you will see in Table A.5, the couple needs **$165,000 after-tax savings!** Since the couple's saving are in a traditional IRA, which is before taxes, they need $220,000 in their IRA. Table A.5 shows how the couple's savings will support their needs for 23 years, which will get them to age 93. Unless you really want to, there is no reason for you to go through this table in great detail. It is included only so you can get some idea of funds flow and some appreciation of how income and expense numbers get huge when inflation is accounted for.

The years shown in Table A.5 start at the first year of retirement.

If the couple had *not* had their home paid for, they would have had to add the amount they owed on their home to the required savings. For example, if this couple had a $100,000 mortgage, they would have needed $165,000 + $100,000 = $265,000 in after-tax savings to retire.

One more adjustment will be of interest for those few people who have a fixed company pension. This couple did not have a company pension, but if they did, the required savings could have been reduced by the amount of the annual after-tax pension multiplied by 13. So, if the couple had a $10,000 after-tax annual pension scheduled to start at age 65, the couple could have reduced their required savings by $130,000. This would have made the required savings $165,000 – $130,000 = $35,000. With a $10,000 *inflation-adjusted* after-tax pension that was originally scheduled to start at age 65, the required savings could have been reduced by the amount of the annual after-tax pension multiplied by 20. This would have made the required savings $165,000 – $200,000. This negative number means the couple required no additional savings beyond their pension to support their retirement.

Additional Detail on How Savings Were Calculated

The following is for the very few people who want to know even more detail on how the book's values were determined. For most people, it will bring on a headache!

TABLE A.5 Savings Flow, Above-Average Wage Couple, 70 Years Old, Retiring Soon

Year	Start of Year Savings	Income on Savings	Social Security Income	Total Income	Retirement Expenses	End of Year Savings
1	$165,000	$10,725	$29,750	$40,475	$40,000	$165,475
2	$165,475	$10,756	$30,791	$41,547	$41,400	$165,622
3	$165,622	$10,765	$31,869	$42,634	$42,849	$165,408
4	$165,408	$10,751	$32,984	$43,736	$44,349	$164,795
5	$164,795	$10,712	$34,139	$44,850	$45,901	$163,744
6	$163,744	$10,643	$35,334	$45,977	$47,507	$162,214
7	$162,214	$10,544	$36,570	$47,114	$49,170	$160,158
8	$160,158	$10,410	$37,850	$48,261	$50,891	$157,527
9	$157,527	$10,239	$39,175	$49,414	$52,672	$154,269
10	$154,269	$10,027	$40,546	$50,574	$54,516	$150,327
11	$150,327	$ 9,771	$41,965	$51,737	$56,424	$145,640
12	$145,640	$ 9,467	$43,434	$52,901	$58,399	$140,141
13	$140,141	$ 9,109	$44,954	$54,063	$60,443	$133,762
14	$133,762	$ 8,695	$46,528	$55,222	$62,558	$126,426
15	$126,426	$ 8,218	$48,156	$56,374	$64,748	$118,052
16	$118,052	$ 7,673	$49,842	$57,515	$67,014	$108,553
17	$108,553	$ 7,056	$51,586	$58,642	$69,359	$ 97,836
18	$ 97,836	$ 6,359	$53,392	$59,751	$71,787	$ 85,800
19	$ 85,800	$ 5,577	$55,260	$60,837	$74,300	$ 72,338
20	$ 72,338	$ 4,702	$57,194	$61,896	$76,900	$ 57,334
21	$ 57,334	$ 3,727	$59,196	$62,923	$79,592	$ 40,665
22	$ 40,665	$ 2,643	$61,268	$63,911	$82,377	$ 22,199
23	$ 22,199	$ 1,443	$63,412	$64,855	$85,260	$ 1,794
24	$ 1,794	$ 117	$65,632	$65,749	$88,245	−$ 20,702

Example: A 50-year-old single individual, with an above-average wage ($50,000 to $90,000) and $50,000 in current after-tax retirement savings, wants to retire in 15 years at age 65. He or she is planning on a $13,333 fixed pension that is projected to start at age 65 and wants a retirement income with a current value of $30,000 after taxes.

The first thing to do is see what these values will look like in 15 years, assuming 3.5 percent inflation (which is the historical average).

We will assume that the $50,000 savings is in TIPS paying 3 percent per year. The value of the savings also goes up with inflation, so the total yield is 3 percent + 3.5 percent = 6.5 percent. We want to multiply $50,000 times 1.065 each year for 15 years, which is $50,000*1.065^15 = $128,592. So, the current savings, with earnings and inflation included, will be **$128,592** in 15 years.

The pension is a different story. Companies generally quote a pension in the before-tax dollars you will get at age 65, which in this case is $13,333. However, we want the after-tax value, which we will assume is 75 percent times $13,333 = **$10,000** in 15 years.

We want a retirement after-tax income equivalent to $30,000 in current dollars. We will have to inflate this value at 3.5 percent per year for 15 years, which is $30,000*1.035^15 = $50,260. So we want an actual after-tax retirement income of **$50,260** in 15 years.

The only reason to know current wage income is to determine the amount of Social Security. The tables have three levels of Social Security. It was stated that this individual is in the above-average wage level (a current before-tax salary of $50,000 to $90,000), which will earn approximately $19,200 Social Security in current dollars. However, since Social Security is adjusted up with inflation, we look at its value **20 years from now.** Note that we look at 20 years from now, rather than 15 years from now, because the book assumes that Social Security will be delayed until age 70. This means that, for the first five years of retirement, this retiree will *not* be getting Social Security. Now, for the inflated value of Social Security: $19,200*1.035^20 = **$38,204** in 20 years. So, at age 65, the retiree will have $128,592 in savings and a pension of $30,000 per year. Once he reaches 70, his Social Security of $38,204 will kick in. However, since Social Security is subject to income tax, we assume a 15 percent reduction for taxes.

Ignoring the retiree's current savings for now, we want to calculate how much initial *total* savings he would need at the start of retirement such that he could draw out his desired retirement income of $50,260, which will index up every year with inflation. We want the funds to run out at age 93, which is 28 years from the time he retires.

We will look at this one year at a time. On a spreadsheet, we will start out guessing at an initial total savings amount and then adjust the required total savings amount up or down such that the funds run out in 28 years. Here are word formulas describing what we are going to look at every year. The earnings yields and inflation are assumed to be in decimals.

- Funds Value, End of Year 1: (Initial total savings times (expected earnings yield + inflation)) + pension – (retirement income plus inflation).

- Funds Value, End of Year 2: (Total savings at end of first year times (expected earnings yield + inflation)) + pension – (retirement income from first year plus inflation).

- Funds Value, End of Years 3, 4, and 5: continue as previously.

- Funds Value, End of Year 6: (Total savings at end of fifth year times (expected earnings + inflation)) + pension + inflated Social Security – (retirement income from fifth year plus inflation).

- Funds Value, End of Years 7 through 28: Continue as previously with the goal of having the total savings value at the end of year 28 equal to zero. Keep adjusting the initial total savings guess until the total savings value at the end of year 28 is close to zero.

Note that the total savings value cannot be allowed to go below zero at any time before age 93. In some incidences, the minimum initial savings amount is dictated by how much is needed to get to the time where Social Security, or pension, kicks in, rather than at the end of the 28 years.

If we do this example calculation for initial total savings using the future values we derived for pension, Social Security, and retirement income, we get a total savings requirement in 15 years of **$446,869.** Note that one of the reasons this number looks so high is because it includes expected inflation for the next 15 years. In current dollars, it would be much less.

Once we have the initial total savings guess finalized, we then look at how much of the total required savings is covered by the initial savings amount. Since we calculated that the future value of the current $50,000 savings (including yield and inflation) is $128,592, we subtract this amount from the $446,869 total savings: $446,869 – $128,592 = **$318,277.**

We now want to calculate how much we have to save every year to accumulate the extra $318,277 we will need at retirement. We want the savings amount to feel the same every year, so we want it to index up every year with inflation. Also, the savings we accumulate as the years go by will be earning 3 percent yields and increasing 3.5 percent every year with assumed inflation, for a total of 6.5 percent. These are the same numbers we assumed earlier with our TIPS investment.

To calculate this annual savings amount for our example:

Annual savings = $318,277/(1.065^14 + 1.065^13*1.035^1 + 1.065^12*1.035^2+ $\cdots$ +1.065^1*1.035^13 + 1.035^14)

Annual savings = **$10,651,** which will index up with inflation each year for the 15 years until age 65.

Comparing these results with what would have been obtained with the earlier chapter tables:

Nominal annual savings = $19,219

Minus correction for prior savings: $4,250

Minus correction for fixed pension: $4,300

So, $19,219 – $4,250 – $4300 = $10,669, which is essentially the same as the $10,651 we calculated before.

Glossary

Actively Managed Mutual Funds: These investments combine money from many investors into a fund that actively analyzes and buys stocks, bonds, and other assets.

Bins: In a histogram, the total range of data is split into equal range-proportioned sized spaces, or "bins."

Bubble: When an asset's price rises so high that it becomes extremely overvalued by any reasonable economic measure.

Certificates of Deposit (CDs): Similar to a savings account at a bank, except that the depositor agrees to keep the money in the account for a specified period of time; CDs pay higher interest rates than savings accounts, but they have a penalty for early withdrawal.

Chief Financial Officer (CFO): The executive responsible for the financial aspects of the company.

Chi-Square Test: A test done to check a population's sigma against a sample's sigma.

Consumer Price Index (CPI): A measure of the cost of goods purchased by an average U.S. family.

Correlations: Historical data are used to see if an investment variable changed at the same time on different investments or if multiple investment variables changed at the same time on one investment.

Cumulative Function: A specific function within Excel that sums the probabilities of something happening a given number of times *or less*.

Cumulative Probability: The summed probabilities of multiple outcomes up to and including a given number.

Current Dividend: The most recent share of profits received by a shareholder, usually stated on an annual basis.

Dividends: A distribution of corporate earnings.

Dollar Averaging: Buying a specific dollar amount of stock each month mathematically makes the average price of the stock purchased lower than the overall average price of the stock, because fewer shares are bought when the stock price is high and more shares are bought when the stock price is low.

DR: The yield we expect from the stock market to make it an investment we would choose over a safer alternative investment.

Excel's BINOMDIST: This is the Excel tool used to determine the probability of a proportional data result due to pure random chance.

Exchange Traded Funds (ETFs):   Funds that track an index but can be traded like a stock.

F Test: Checks for a statistically significant change in variables data sigmas when comparing two samples.

Financial Obligations Ratio: The ratio of monthly payments versus after-tax income.

Fixed Market Basket: An identical basket of goods whose cost change represents the rate of inflation.

Gauge Error: How much of the allowable error (tolerance) is taken up by errors in the measurement method itself

Gross Domestic Product: The total value of all the goods and services produced in a country in a given year.

Hedonistic Adjustment of Price Data: Assumes that the cost of any improvement in a product should be discounted when compared with an earlier price.

Histogram: A bar graph that is a display of tabulated frequencies.

Home Equity: The value of a home minus the amount owed on the home.

Index Funds: Enable investors to buy stocks in the same balance as in a particular index, with no attempt to evaluate the individual merits of each stock within the index.

IRA, Regular: Money is saved pretax, and all taxes are paid when the funds are withdrawn, generally after age 59½; taxes are then paid not only on the funds deposited but also on any gains those funds have generated.

IRA, Roth: Taxes are paid up front on the funds as they are being saved, and there are no additional taxes on those funds or on any related gains when the funds are withdrawn, generally after age 59½.

Irving Fisher Formula: A numerical way to determine a fair market value of a stock or the stock market in general.

Key Process Input Variables (KPIVs):   The main drivers affecting change; the stock market, and even a small business, has many contributing elements, but it is important to concentrate on the KPIVs.

Logarithmic Charting: On a logarithmic chart (actually semilog), the vertical axis is spaced equivalent to the power of the plotted number.

Market Timing: Attempting to buy at a stock's low price and sell at its high.

Market Value: The calculated fair price of a stock or stocks, a number that provides a reasonable baseline against which to evaluate a stock's price.

Minimum Sample Size: The number of data points needed for a statistically valid comparison.

Money Managers: Managers who emphasize optimizing quarterly profits rather than other aspects of running or building a company.

Mutual Funds: Combine money from many investors into a fund that actively analyzes and buys stocks, bonds, and other investments.

Normal Distribution: A bell-shaped distribution of data that is indicative of many things in nature, including much of the data related to investments.

Number s: The number of "successes" that you are looking for in a probability problem using Excel's BINOMDIST.

Pension: A sum of money regularly paid as a retirement benefit.

Plot Data: Plot shapes of investment data often stay similar unless a major change in that investment has occurred. If a major shape change occurs, it is often of interest. Numerical tests are not appropriate for comparing data before and after such a data shape change.

Population Data: A large number of data points collected over an extended period of time.

Price/Dividend Ratio: The stock price divided by the annual dividend paid on that share of stock.

Price/Earnings Ratio: The stock price divided by its annual, after-tax, per-share earnings.

Probability: The likelihood or chance of an event happening due to pure chance.

Probability P (or Probability s):   The likelihood of a random "success" on an individual trial, like the likelihood of a "head" on a coin flip, which is 0.5.

Proportional Data: Often have just two levels of discrimination, like qualitative comparisons of more or less, true or false, and higher or lower.

Quantitative Statistical Techniques: A method of collecting, analyzing, and interpreting data, with emphasis on numerical statistical analysis.

Random Walk Theory on Stocks: At any given time, a stock price is just as likely to go up or down, and whatever price a stock has at any moment is the best consensus price of all investors, including all the rumors and expectations of the future.

Real Price: Price without any adjustment for the effect of inflation.

Regression to the Mean Theory: Assumes that if a stock, or the stock market in general, is higher priced than it generally was in the past, and there is no known reason that it should be higher priced, then the price of the stock or stock market is more likely to go down than up.

Seasonal Change: Predictable changes that are caused by annual events and therefore not indicative of any real long-term change.

Short Selling: Selling a stock you do not own because you think the price of the stock is going to fall; to do this, by means of your broker, you borrow the stock from an existing owner, sell it, and buy it back later (you hope at a lower price), so you can return the stock to its original owner.

Six Sigma: A problem-solving methodology that uses data to drive decisions.

Social Security: A U.S. federal program that includes retirement benefits.

Splits: A company increases the number of its shares, and the price then adjusts downward in the same proportion; the net equity of each shareholder after a stock split generally stays the same.

Standard Deviation (or Sigma): A measure of the variation of values within a group of numbers: the more uniform and consistent the numbers, the lower the sigma, and the more variation within the group of numbers, the larger the sigma.

Stock Index: A measure of the performance of a select group of companies.

Stock Index Fund: Enables investors to buy stocks in the same balance as the stocks in a particular index.

t **test:** Checks for a statistically significant change in variables data averages when comparing a sample and a population or comparing two samples.

Treasury Inflation Protected Securities (TIPS): A low-risk, conservative investment that automatically adjusts for inflation, an investment choice that is especially good for anyone who is concerned about high inflation or a possible stock market crash.

Variables Data: Usually given as decimals and can have almost infinite resolution; generally the most valuable type of data.

Index